WE ARE THE CAT

Also by Terry Bain

YOU ARE A DOG

WE ARE THE CAT

Life Through the Eyes of the
Royal Feline

TERRY BAIN

Harmony Books
NEW YORK

Copyright © 2006 by Terry Bain

Published in the United States by Harmony Books,
an imprint of the Crown Publishing Group,
a division of Random House, Inc., New York.
www.crownpublishing.com

Harmony Books is a registered trademark and the Harmony Books
colophon is a trademark of Random House, Inc.

Library of Congress Cataloging-in-Publication Data

Bain, Terry.
We are the cat : life through the eyes of the royal feline/
Terry Bain.—1st ed.
p. cm.
1. Cats. I. Title.
SF445.5.B35 2006
599.75—dc22 2006004984

ISBN-13: 978-0-307-33918-8
ISBN-10: 0-307-33918-1

Printed in the United States of America

Design by Lynne Amft

10 9 8 7 6 5 4 3 2 1

First Edition

Sarah

ACKNOWLEDGMENTS

I will try to keep this simple.

The hardest part (for me) of writing a book is clearing away the important things in life (like my wife and kids, my cat and dogs) and making room and time to be still and write the darn book. I could not do this without my love, Sarah, and my children. Thank you for helping make my life extraordinary.

Thank you to the editors at Harmony, Kim and Shaye, for believing in me and my ridiculous books about cats and dogs. And thank you to superagent Jenny Bent . . . you simply rock.

And finally, the cat. She will not allow me to finish my acknowledgments without thanking her. And so be it. Thank you, Swiper. Without you . . . well, I would not have been pulled from bed so early yesterday to clean up whatever that was outside the bathroom door. I assume there is some blessing to be taken from being allowed to do so. Right now I can't think of what it is, and maybe that will be the topic of another book at another time.

Until that time, blessings and thanks to all of you.

CONTENTS

CONTENTS

OUR FOREWORD
(AS TOLD TO THE AUTHOR)

When we first heard that the author of this book—or, as we sometimes refer to him, Scratch—was writing about us, we were nonplussed. But then we gave it some thought. Some timely and careful consideration. And we have come to the following conclusions.

We are not inclined to allow him to write a book about us. We have been watching him and reading what he's written so far—the book about dogs and such, with references to us scattered about—and we do not entirely approve. We also wonder why on earth he would choose to write about *dogs* before writing about *cats;* this we feel speaks directly to his character, and we therefore must assume that he is more seriously flawed than we previously thought. So, no, he should not write this book.

It isn't that we don't agree with much of what he has

written about dogs (though what we have read makes little sense to us. We understand *reading,* and *language,* but the sense it makes is much like dogs themselves—that is, not much sense at all). We hope that should he write a book about us, we will not be made the butt of his jokes. We are in favor of people knowing us better so as to be left alone more often (when we want to be left alone), or appreciated as we should be (when we want to be appreciated). But we are not in favor of a book that does not take us seriously, or that paints a picture of us that is untoward, or that is otherwise not written by a cat. He is not a cat, and therefore should not be allowed to write such a book, no matter how seriously he writes about us, no matter how catlike he seems to be at times (or doglike, as it were, which we think should disqualify him altogether). We do not wish him to speak for us. We will speak for ourselves. And we will therefore take the matter of what sort of book he *is* allowed to write into consideration. Maybe a book about humans. Is he not a human?

Despite our efforts, he has continued to write this book. Did we not ask him to stop? Did we not say that we were not inclined to allow him to write a book about us, and we would think about it and get back to him? Did we not say that he was certainly better suited for writing something else? About himself? About Sitting and Warming Chairs? Is he not paying attention? We asked that he put that Ridiculous Machine away (though the Ridiculous Machine is very warm, at times, and therefore Useful to Cats). And open the door. We would like to go Out of Doors and have a rest on the porch, in the sun, so that we might observe the activities of those still Indoors, from behind glass, through the front window. And when we return, we will be asking that all documents associated with this book be either turned over to us or destroyed immediately.

He is obviously not listening.

We suggest he stop writing this ridiculous book and come let us out before it is too late. We have to go out. Does he not know this? We cannot open the door by ourselves. Come let us out. Or install a cat door, like the one they have across this street.

Immediately.

Still, he continues.

We have decided that in the end we cannot prevent him from doing what it is he is doing. We have a certain amount of power in the household and can control a certain number of the activities that occur here, but we have little control over what Scratch writes on that (now extremely warm) machine. And though we still do not approve, we must allow him to carry on. In return he has allowed us this space to notify the reading public of our complaint, of our disapproval of what he has done.

We will also be allowed this: When he is away from his desk, we will walk across the keyboard, we will lie upon the computer monitor, and we will swipe at the fish that sometimes live behind the screen. This is our prerogative, as this book is, apparently, his.

Finally, despite our hesitation, we hope that you enjoy the book.

I

WEDENTITY

We do not have the same difficulty with human language that many creatures do, so we understand when they call us Cat or Kitty or Swiper or Tigger that they mean this to be a name for us. (Also Toby or Smokey or Hadley.) What we have trouble with is informing the people of our household that we do not consider this to be Our Name. (Levi? Maddie? Sandra? No. No. And no.) In fact, we generally consider ourselves nameless, except for the one indescribable mark of our scent. (Not Josie. Not Leopard. Not Owl.) This one scent, the Us that is *us,* is how we identify one another, and how we identify Other Creatures, so a wordname is particularly meaningless.

We will sometimes respond to our "name," of course (Dave, Creature, Patch) as it pleases or benefits us. There are times when our name means "feeding time" or "the door is open," or even "this is absolutely the last time I am calling for you before I go upstairs and utterly forget cats exist."

For the sake of simplicity (because this is intended to be a Human Text rather than a Cat Text), we will give the humans of our household humanlike names. We understand they have names of a sort that they use among themselves, but we have trouble keeping track of these names because they make no real sense in the real world and are given to them before they even open their eyes. (How is it possible to name your young before knowing who they are, before knowing how they act or smell?)

For example, *Terry* is a name, but what does it mean? We understand it means *something* in human language, but it makes no sense as a name. What is the meaning behind the word *Terry* other than "the human that is called *Terry* for no better reason than to have something to call him"? Would he not be better suited to a name such as Tallest Though Sitting or Smells of Butter and Coffee? But they do not call him this. They call him *Terry*. We think this is confusing and that it would be better to call him nothing at all.

So we will refer to the humans in the following ways.

We will give all the humans specific names that actually mean something for the sake of keeping them separate from one another, so you will be able to follow our line of thought. They will be Scratch and Mom and Kittengirl and Fly. Reasonable descriptions of these names follow in the proceeding sections.

Some more general names: For the most part, the tall, hairless creatures in our household (sometimes known as *humans*) have a few very important qualities, the most noticeable of which is their ability to sit in such a way as to provide a lap, and when they do so, of course, that lap provides warmth. We therefore refer to them, in general, as Laps (plural) or Lap (singular), or sometimes Our Lap, if we want to indicate a greater attachment to a given Lap, especially when they are sitting, prone, awaiting our presence. So warm, this lap. So soft and full of peace.

More on the qualities of lapness later. For now, simply know that if you are of the species that is able to produce a lap, this is one of the great and honorable ways we think of you. And we honor you, of course, with the courtesy of lying there while napping. Lucky for you to have a lap. Lucky for you your lap is warm. Skilled you may be at some other, unknown task, but your greatest quality is simply a matter of luck.

S C R A T C H

Scratch is what we call the male adult Lap of our household. He pretends, at times, to be of some importance, to rule or to control. But there is little in the household that he actually rules or controls. Perhaps he rules and controls the extremely noisy and irritating car that nobody ever drives or rides in but him. We do not know.

He does seem to know exactly where and how to scratch behind our ears, and at what depth and duration. We rarely have to warn him that we are finished with his scratch, and when we do warn him, or when we bat away his hand or bite, he does not seem to mind.

Also he scratches just near our tail, and on our haunches above the knee. He scratches in a way that we are not able to scratch, but nevertheless seems natural, as if this is a scratch that was Meant to Be, and it is one of the Reasons We Are Here. We therefore call him Scratch.

M o m

We have heard the children call their mother Mom or Mama or even Moms, and these are all sensible sounds. Mom is the sort of nonsense word we can understand, because it makes sense as a sound alone, and it is a sound we can nearly make. Our vocalization of *mother* sounds a bit more like *Meoam* than *Mom,* but we appreciate being able to use a name for her that both makes sense and that is used by Lap children. Furthermore, it resembles what we called our own mother before we were able to open our eyes and we needed to call out for her. "Meeum. Meeum."

Not exactly, but as close as any of our vocalizations come to Lap language.

We wonder if this is a universal name for Mother that originates from something essential about what a mother is or does. More from emotion, from a soothing touch rather than a thought. A mother is: Mom, Mam, Meeum, Mama, Mum. Mmm. *Murr.*

Furthermore, Mom most closely approaches the essential feline of all the people in our household. She sometimes reminds us of a Catmother. When she calls us, we keep our distance, and when she is concentrating elsewhere (ah, she is reading the newspaper), we demand her attention. She returns this attitude by similarly turning away from us when we demand her attention, and coming toward us, ready to pour on the attention, when we are otherwise occupied (usually asleep).

When we enter a room, Mom often calls out to us, "Aw, Kitty," in an affectionate tone, a voice that says, "We know you will not come closer, but if you wanted to come closer, you could come closer and receive appropriate attention, but we also know, because we are very much like you, that you want to be elsewhere, so do not feel as if you need to come closer. We're here when you need us."

She is wise. Able to communicate so much with so little. Like us. And now that we think about it, though she is a Lap, she is quite beautiful. How is that possible?

We will examine this beauty later, when she is sleeping. We will lie close to her face and watch her breathing, to see if that beauty is still there, or if it is something she puts on for our benefit. We expect the former. No beauty such as this could be easily manufactured. It is likely something much deeper.

Could it be that she is also expecting a litter of kittens?

Perhaps. And she is not watching us now. So we sit near the bathroom door and admire her. Waiting to be fed.

"Meoam," we say, and by this we mean Mom.

FLY

The elder child is a male of the Lap species who seems, at times, to fly. He does so in much the same way that most earthbound creatures fly—that is, his feet may leave the ground, and he may cross great distances while his feet have left the ground, but he will eventually return to ground before leaping off again. It is the sort of flight that is actually neither flight nor glide. His flight reminds us of the sheepherding dogs that run headlong into whatever joy there is to be had in any direction they might find it. The second dog of the household (which we call Daydog) is just one of these dogs. Her feet may touch the ground, but she is nevertheless in flight.

The elder Lap child is a flyer in the sense of movement across the ground and over the sofa and through the living room (a cat should always be aware of his position so as not to be stepped on or stumbled over), so we call him Fly.

For the most part he ignores us, or warns the younger child against lifting or lying on us, and we appreciate the mastery of his will. He is apparently controlling his desire to touch and pet and be near us, and we therefore will, at times, go near him. He may pet us for a moment. Just long enough. Just perfect. Utterly remarkable how he resists us.

Just the scent of him soothes us. During the day, we can often be found sleeping on his bed.

KITTENGIRL

The younger child of our Lap family is female, and kittenlike, in her way. She moves unpredictably. She is a catlifter. She will often lift us for no better reason than to lift a cat, it seems, or to move a cat to a space where a cat does not wish to be. When she lifts us, it is best not to struggle. We hang from her embrace like a coat, and when she reaches the place where she intended us to be, she will set us down and we are then allowed to flee.

"Careful of the kitty," says Scratch. Too late, of course.

It should be noted that Kittengirl is most likely already

being "careful," but her care is different than what Scratch means by the word *careful,* or full of care, and thus we experience some discomfort and wish not to be lifted or moved in this way.

Her actions, of course, are every bit as much like those of a kitten as they could be for a Lap, so we call her Kittengirl.

"I *am* being careful," says Kittengirl. And of course, as we thought, she is. Very careful indeed. She cannot help acting as she does, just as a kitten cannot help acting as a kitten does.

We avoid her most times (as we might sometimes avoid a kitten). We sometimes wonder why, when avoiding her, we seem to miss being thus lifted.

NIGHTDOG

The giant black dog who lived in this house before we arrived (and who used to interact with us, before the appearance of Daydog, at which time there was an apparent shift of roles in the household), we call Nightdog. She is black like the night, and when it is dark outside, she disappears in the darkness. This is a talent we did not know dogs could possess. We were sure invisibility was a quality reserved for cats. But Nightdog can do it, whether she uses the same technique as us or not. For this, we respect her. In response to our respectfulness, she tends to ignore us.

DAYDOG

The second dog, who appeared in the household several months after us and who seems to believe it is her duty to teach us to be a sheep, we call Daydog. She is white with black markings, but it is not her coloring that gives her this name. She is scentmarked with the day, with sunlight and activity. She does not ever stop moving, except to sleep (and she sleeps mostly at night, while staying active and full of motion during the day). She attempts to herd us throughout the house, moving us in one direction or another, and she bites at our neck and head as if this will encourage us to move in a particular direction. When she bites at our neck and head, this does not encourage us to do anything but attempt to extract our head from her mouth.

We believe Daydog needs a second job. Perhaps she could mow lawns or drive a delivery truck. (Of course we know this is not within her ability. Did you think cats did not have a sense of humor?) There is too much energy in Daydog's slight body to be wasted tormenting us. Get her out of the house, we say. Let her contribute something to the household besides anxiety. There must be a use for all this energy.

If we could only teach her to open the door when we wanted in or out. That would be her ideal position. She would likely be willing to do it all day long, at the exact moment we asked her to.

This is a stroke of brilliance, of course, and has occurred to us just this moment. We will begin to train her at once.

THE ONLY CAT IN THE WORLD

We understand we are not the only cat in the world. We know of Othercats. (We have even seen Othercats in the box known as the Television, via which is delivered all things worth knowing.) And we understand that some cats do not necessarily think in the same way that we do. But we do not feel the need to complicate this knowledge with a great deal of respect for the thoughts and activities of the Othercats. We have no trouble speaking for Othercats or acting as if we actually are the only cat in the world. We have no trouble speaking, indeed, for anyone at any time, be they cats or humans or antelopes. And we understand that Othercats may do the same for us. And they likely will. They likely are driven by the same impulses and prejudices as we are.

When Laps begin to understand this about us, their lives will become much easier.

CATFAMILY

We live with humans (Laps). We've lived with them almost as long as we can remember. We remember Other Creatures, of course, but Laps have been imprinted on us for a very long time, and though we know, logically, that they cannot be of the same genetic makeup as feline-beings, we nevertheless consider them Family. We are adaptable to almost any creature, and though Laps are odd and large creatures, they are Just Feline Enough to be considered Catfamily (especially Mom, who, as we said, is very nearly felinekind to begin with).

Other creatures we have considered Catfamily, when familiarity and intimacy require it (usually when said creatures are Taken In and Adopted by our Laps) are quite varied: Dogs, Bears, Squirrels (very rare), Sheep, Ducks,

Moose, Snakes, Raccoons, Marmots (extremely rare), Lemurs, et cetera. Very few reptiles and no insects make the list (even when adopted by our Laps). It is not that we have anything against reptiles and insects per se. It is just that we prefer a creature that can offer us something in the way of heat should we decide to snuggle down for a nap with them. Even large reptiles do not have any heat to share with us. In fact, they seem to steal it from us, so it is a very rare cat indeed that considers a snake or other reptile a member of its family.

Many of these creatures, had we not known them before their becoming Catfamily, would instead be Prey. And, if not Prey, then Enemies of the Crown. Individual needs of individual cats are assessed on an individual basis. We think this should be obvious, but some still seem surprised when an individual cat accepts an individual dog, for instance, as both companion and family. Especially Laps seem surprised at this. They should not be so surprised. True, many, if not most, dogs are considered Enemies of the Crown, but do Laps not live with both dogs and cats? Do they not live with Bears and Squirrels and Sheep and Ducks? Laps are not so different from us when it comes to their ability to consider many species as members of their family.

As we have said before of our Lap Catfamily, they are

Just Feline Enough. This is much to their great benefit, as Felinity is the path to inner peace (and peace, both Inner and Outer, is a Preferable State of Being for creatures who wish to spend their lives with a cat).

OTHERCATS

Cats outside the family are what we call Othercats. Othercats are much like us, and if we want to know anything about Othercats we can look inside ourselves to see what it is that makes them who they are. When we do this, we are sympathetic, but we are also cautious. We know that an approaching Othercat may have an ulterior motive in his approach. It may be that he is attempting to expand his territory (especially true of Tomcats), and this is not allowed.

Mating with Othercats: Queen Point of View

It may also be that a Tomcat is interested in mating, and we know enough about mating to know it is not at all for us (even though, given the right circumstances, we understand we will not be able to help ourselves). Tomcats have, it seems, some positive, though indescribable, qualities that keep us from marking them forever as Enemies of the

Crown. It is unfortunate that this is so, because we are convinced that without them our lives would be much simpler.

Mating with Othercats: Tom Point of View

Simpler?

We do not know exactly what it is that has caused such a hostile proclamation from the Queens. We are every bit as capable of diplomacy as they (though we admit to carrying out our diplomacy in a very different manner), but certain advances must be made to carry forward the genetic superiority of our species. Would they even notice us if we did not make fools of ourselves? We think they would not, and the cat species would therefore perish.

And anyway, did they not want kittens? We are relatively certain that they did. Otherwise, why go scentmarking their territory the way they do? They claim not to be scentmarking in order to attract a Tom, but we are plain certain this is utter humbug.

Neighborhood Othercats

There are several Othercats that seem to live in our neighborhood, many of whom cross into our territory. We discourage this by scentmarking and prowling and standing guard upon the fencetop, but it continues nonetheless.

There are also several Othercats that live exclusively in neighborhood households. They almost never leave their houses. It is more difficult to know them either by scent or sight, because they are generally not to be seen Out of Doors.

Across the street, for instance, there are two Othercats, each of whom we sometimes see in the front window, apparently resting on the back of a sofa, longing for the motion that occurs beyond the glass (this motion is imagined, based on our own experience of sitting on the back of the sofa, longing for that same motion). We have attempted to visit these cats, and will wait on their front steps to be let Indoors, but we have not as of yet been able to pass into their house. At times when the door has been opened, one of the Othercats is either waiting near the door to escape or has been picked up by one of the Laps who lives there (there are two Laps, both female), in order to prevent escape.

Once in a great while this Othercat (the gray one who looks much larger than she probably is, who we sometimes think of as Desire, as she seems like pure desire . . . to escape . . . to experience the Out of Doors for herself) manages to trick the Laps and escape into the Out of Doors. As with many Indoor cats, once Desire is Out of Doors, she does not quite know what to do with herself. The Out of Doors can be an overwhelming experience for an Indoor cat—so much so that her body will shut down, lying itself in the grass near the neighbor's fence, attempting to process the stream of sensory information as it presents itself to her in a kind of frenzy unlike anything she can experience Indoors: bird, wind, grass, cool, moist, tree, sky, bird, moth, Lap, shape, car, shadow, door, flower, skateboard, dog, bird, mosquito, bird, fence, bird, echo, bird, music, bird.

If she spent enough time in the Out of Doors, she would likely be quite comfortable there, and her desire would diminish. But the processing time in the grass is usually at least long enough for a Lap to notice that she has escaped, so she is found and lifted and returned to the house, an Indoor cat once more.

It is likely best this way. At least inside the house she is in no danger of being trampled by buffalo.

2

GROWTH AND DISCOVERY

We begin as creatures known by Laps as kittens or kits or kitties, and though kittens very much resemble miniature versions of adult cats, they are not the same (exactly). They are like precursors of us. They are not inferior, but different, and as we grow older, we change, we discover, we become what we are today, which means that though kittens can be persistent and annoying and aggressive and cute and passionate and willful and overzealous and stubborn and maddening and precious and bothersome, these are all admirable qualities that many of us hope to carry with us into adulthood, so kittens should therefore be respected as cats in the making.

Also (and perhaps obviously), kittens are great fun to watch.

NEWBORN

The world is dark and we wiggle against the warmth, against the further wiggle, the soft mewling sound of siblings, of further darkness, and we wonder if we will be fed again, and if we will be fed again how it is we will find the food, the place to go for the food, for this moment we do not smell the food, do not hear the food, do not know where the food has gone. The milk. Where is the milk?

But then there is the scent approaching, so closely to when we were just thinking that we needed it, and there is the soft thrumming noise of the milk, of the Mother, the *trrrr rrrrr purr* that is the sound of filling us up with warmth, and we try to move toward it and the warm warm paw paw mother draws us in somehow, wraps us into her belly, and we push against the softness with our paws, wiggle against the milk and suck our way into the fullness, all full of light. This is where the light comes from. This we know for sure.

We are One Kitten, and we listen. We are able to listen to whatever it is we cannot see, and we can listen with the assistance of our siblings. We are listening for *warm;* we encircle one another without "nose" and without "tail," just kitten turned around, kitten asleep and a mother there surrounding kitten, somewhere, abounding. When we eventually open our eyes and see, the sight will be secondary to our sense of Kitten, of Litter, of Mother. To see all of this best we will close our eyes and see with nose and tongue and whisker and ear. We see memory. We see. That one brilliant light. From everywhere.

Q U E E N   M O T H E R

We are full of the pressure and want them to be near now so the pressure and the *trrrr rrrrr purr* comes automatically as it hasn't quite before now and we go to where they are and lie near and continue the *trrrr rrrrr purr* and they wiggle toward and away and toward us. We draw them in toward us, the sound and heat and scent of the milk in us, and they find us and push against us with their paws and push and all push and suck, the milk is moving finally moving, and yes we feel the pressure pass, the pressure move from us into them. Is that all it took? Finally, some release.

For a while. In a while it will be too light. Too intense. And we will get up even before they seem finished, even before they stop pushing their paws against us and taking milk, still desperate for milk, because suddenly it seems as if the world is touching us, as if the room is too small, as if the sofa has moved three feet closer, as if the house itself is all doors and all the doors are closed, as if the curtains are all drawn, as if it is anyway too too light to see, even with all the doors and windows closed, so we have to move away from them and they will play for a moment, blind but playful. Then sleep. As the doors all pull away and open. As the light dims down to bearable brightness, we too will sleep. Close enough to hear them, to smell. But far enough to keep the doors at a safe distance. And open just a crack.

M I M S

When we were still a kitten we left our mother and set off on our own to become a part of our Lap family. When we arrived in our new household, we still found that we had a strong desire to suckle, and we therefore sought out appropriate means of satisfying this need. We tried Kitten-girl's hair (this was, of course, before we minded being lifted, so suckling her hair seemed safe), and we tried strands of the carpet and tassels hanging from tables, but we were unsatisfied until we found the Mims. We realized even then that the Mims was a Humanchild toy, something to snuggle with at night and encourage good dreams, but we did not realize until later that the Mims was, in fact, in the shape of a dog.

By then, of course, it was too late. This was our Mims and our Mims was the best and only Mims in all the world. There has never been such an excellent Mims ever, and we knead the Mims as we would a Catmother and we nurse on the Mims's long hair and we curl ourselves up against the Mims and sleep in the finest dreamland we can imagine (of Mims and Catmother and Full Bellies of Milk). This is, after all, what the Mims is for (comfort and dreamland), and we do not hesitate to make use of it in this way.

C L O W N D O L L

We rub against the Clowndoll because if we do not rub against the Clowndoll, a Dog or Othercat or Lap will think, maybe, it is *theirs,* for it will not have a Recent Scent of Us. But it is *not their Clowndoll.*

We discovered the Clowndoll as we were passing from kittenhood into cathood. We do not nurse on the Clowndoll or knead it or pretend that it is a Catmother (as we do the Mims).

The Clowndoll is not the Mims, and we do not exactly understand our relationship with the Clowndoll, except to say that *it is ours* and we therefore enforce our proprietorship of it as we would any item of the house or of the house itself.

To do so, we rub against it and we sleep near it and *purr* when we are near it. Others may touch it or rub against it or sleep near it or *purr,* but we reclaim it anew each day. Rub against it. Sleep near it. *Purr. Our* Clowndoll. *Ours.*

UPSIDE RIGHT-SIDE

Kittengirl once lifted us and held us so that we were looking at the sky (or the ceiling, anyway, as the sky is somewhere beyond the ceiling and difficult to see when Indoors). But Kittengirl is not always so surehanded, it seems, and suddenly her arms were gone, and as we fell, we were turned upright—our own body responding to the absence of arms, somehow aware of the turning of the earth without our having to tell our body what to do or how to do it—now looking at the floor, standing on the floor, as if we've just pounced on a moving object on the floor. And we have.

A shadow. Pounce.

"Wow! Cool, Kitty. How did you do that?"

At which point Kittengirl lifted us again, turned upside down. And again we are in free fall.

As we fall we think, "Which is upside down and which is right-side up?" But we are unable to answer this question before our feet are on the floor again. *Pounce.* Gravity happens with just this much quickness. And it simply pulls our feet to the ground first. Our feet are more intensely affected by the forces of gravity, just so we can right ourselves this way.

So far as we know, we are the only creatures whose feet are so influenced by gravity.

As we crouch on the floor, Kittengirl shouts for her brother to come watch what she has discovered. So we disappear. Though we are not injured by the activity of falling through the air, neither are we filled with the sort of joy you might expect. Though it takes a great deal of energy to do so, we make ourselves invisible.

WATER

There are many things to know about water. The first and foremost thing to know about water is that we must drink it to survive. A second thing to know (and this is almost as important as the first thing) is that that water is wet. Therefore, though we must drink water in order to live, we must take care. Water is wet, and we've yet to encounter water that is not wet.

We may have mentioned that we do not enjoy wet. In no way do we favor wetness. Wetness is Not for Cats.

Furthermore, though all water is wet, not all water is drinkable. We may be forced to drink undrinkable water (as when we are forced to drink from our cat bowl), but we prefer to drink water that smells like nothing but water. Or we prefer water that smells of the sky or the earth. Or we prefer water that smells of fish and river.

This kind of water is not always available.

Water is produced in our home from a tap, either in the sink or in the bathtub. Some of us prefer to go to the sink and request water there, and some of us prefer to go to the bathtub.

A good time to go to either the sink or the bathtub is when a Lap has gone into the bathroom to use the toilet. We believe the toilet would be a good place from which to drink water (as the dogs sometimes drink water from there), but the water is so low in the bowl that cats drinking from the toilet are in danger of wetness. So long as Laps use the toilet for relieving themselves, however, we will be able to request the use of the taps, and therefore will find drinking from the toilet unnecessary.

When we request water from the tap, a Lap will likely turn the water on low, and we appreciate this, as the water running from the tap reminds us of river water. (Please note that the water is running, not rushing. If you are a Lap and you are reading this, you must know we prefer that the water be dispensed slowly, and we do not appreciate a change in the speed of water as we are drinking from the water, no matter how entertaining this might be to you and those who have gathered to witness our reaction to the rushing water.)

Water from the tap may not smell of river water, but it moves like river water. And any moving water is preferable to unmoving water, as any moving thing, really, has more attraction for us than any nonmoving thing (be it living or nonliving, bird, feather, or bit of string).

We approach and observe the moving water as we approach and observe most moving things. You have seen moving water before, no doubt. Do you not love how the water moves as it runs from the tap? Could you not watch it for hours? And touch . . . a quick flip with our paw (which we know puts us in danger of wetness, but how can we help ourselves?). We could watch the water for many more hours than the average Lap, it seems, because eventually Scratch says to us, "Are you going to get a drink or not?"

We look at him. Did we not come to the bathtub? Did we not request the water?

But first we have to watch the water. What if, when we approach the water to get a drink, it leaps at us? Or, worse, what if it runs away? What if it is unpredictable water? What if it moves away from its path and gets us wet, or disappears altogether?

We bat at the water as if batting at a bird or a fish. (There are no fish in this moving water, which is really too bad. Fish would at least improve on the antiseptic odor of water from the tap.) Batting at the water produces wetness on our paw. We prefer not to have wetness on our paw, so we shake our paw quickly.

Every single time, the water leaps from our paw when we shake it, and it flies into our face. Did we not tell you this was unpredictable water? Did we not tell you that it might act this way?

When the water splashes into our face, we jump back, then away. We go to the bathroom door to lick the water from our paw. Too much wetness is not good for a cat. It is best to remove it as soon as it appears. That way we remove the dangers of wetness before they are real dangers.

We are always thinking ahead. That is why we are the Most Valuable Creatures in a Lap household. It is why we are revered and honored. It is why, after we have escaped the wetness of water from the tap, Scratch realizes the danger he has put us in, and why he turns it off and sighs.

"Whatever," he says.

As you may know, the word *whatever* is a Lap abbreviation for "As you wish."

B O U N C E

As kittens, we had a quality that can only be described as Bounce. Watch a kitten play for approximately three seconds and you will know what we mean by Bounce. We do not exactly have this quality anymore, but because it was not what we would call a useful quality to have—and, indeed, what we would then call Bounce transformed into what we call Pounce today—we do not think of ourselves as having fewer skills now than when we were a kitten. But Bounce was thrilling. When we Bounced, it made us feel as if we had something living inside our belly. Bounce was fun. As an adult cat, fun is difficult to come by. We are so often hunting or patrolling or performing some other duty. These are necessary activities, and they fulfill us, but sometimes we do miss the fun we had as kittens.

N E W   H U N T E R

We wait almost half our lives for the thing we will hunt to appear. We don't know what the thing will be at first. Just that it will appear as we watch the world from behind the fringe of the hanging tablecloth.

This is our territory alone now. These new surroundings. All the siblings, and even the mother, have gone to their own territory. Or rather they stayed in the old territory, and we have been given this one to hunt, to consume, to protect, and to guard. With the fringe and the tablecloth and the light spreading out from the table above. It has been quiet for many seconds. Hundreds of seconds. Not that we are counting. It will be soon.

But wait. The fringe? It moved, didn't it? Is the fringe the hunted thing? Is the fringe what we are to hunt?

It is! It must be! The fringe!

We know because our tail raises automatically and moves slowly, and we are hunched down before the fringe, ready to pounce. The fringe will not escape.

We pounce and birdswipe at the fringe and grab, grab. We've got it! Our claws grip it easily. So easily! It must be the fringe!

Climb and move away, then back and pounce again, birdswipe pounce, leap and grab. Climb up and away and back and pounce and climb; but as we climb, the fringe moves downward to the floor, touching the floor as it hasn't before now.

The sky is falling. The thing that makes the light in the room (our new Laps call it a lamp) is falling from the sky with an enormous crash as we flee, run directionless and away. The thing that made the light in the sky (we will try to remember the word *lamp*) has fallen from the sky, and we do not turn to see what will become of this light, this noise, the world falling around us. We sprint to the kitchen, where there is no traction for a turn, no traction for a stop, and we stop only when we hit the wall at full speed, then ricochet into an open cupboard.

We have learned something. But what? *The fringe was not the hunted.* Perhaps this is what we learned. The fringe is not what we were waiting for. Not prey. The fringe is a kind of hunter, and we do not hunt the hunter. We cannot guarantee that we will not try to hunt the fringe again, but for now we will look for a different thing to hunt from the darkness of the open cupboard.

Something will come by soon.

Perhaps a gazelle.

CATNIP

We don't know exactly what it is about this medicinal herb, but it seems to serve several purposes beyond making an excellent tea for soothing nerves. One of these purposes is to remove all inhibitions from a great number of cats. (Not all cats are affected by catnip in the same way. Experience may, therefore, vary.) Under the influence of catnip, we are not concerned with whoever might see us being just as foolish as we may be, and this is exactly what we become. Foolish. Like a kitten? Yes, like a kitten. We may tumble and grab and pounce and roll as if there is something alive in the catnip. Or something alive just next to the catnip. Or something alive in the next room that must be discovered immediately.

Later we may feel ridiculous for having lost so much control of ourselves, but you will not see it in our demeanor. This is the special ability of a cat. So long as we are not actually inhaling the catnip at the time, we are able to act as if there was never catnip in the universe to make us loopy. Thus, because the universe is whatever we say it is, the catnip may, indeed, not exist at all. Do you have any evidence that catnip exists? We say even the presence of catnip in the bag with CATNIP printed on it does not provide enough evidence of the existence of catnip to categorically declare that there is such a thing.

Until next time, that is, when a bag full of catnip appears in the hallway. Do you see it? We were taken unawares, at first thinking the bag of catnip was nothing more than a small pillow. But when we approached the pillow, we found it to be full of catnip. This is a Lap trick, of course, as they seem to find it entertaining to watch us roll and pounce and arch our backs at the catnip.

Did you see it move? We swear it just moved. There! Look! Did you see that?

When the effects of this catnip wear off, it will again

cease to exist. And when it does? We will exact our revenge.

DOOR

From Indoors

When we are inside the house we are often thinking of the outside, of how many Othercats may be walking through our yard, sitting on our fences, rubbing themselves against our telephone poles, leaving scentmarkings for us to find. We are ready to return Out of Doors to reinvigorate our presence, to leave notice of ourselves upon our outposts, our own scentmarkings and scratchings. So we go to the door and wait at the door and wonder, again, what on earth is the purpose of the door (even an Indoor Cat may do this, sitting and wondering, waiting). Will we ever know the purpose of this obstacle? Would the difference between Out of Doors and Indoors not be apparent even without the door itself? Is not all of what is Indoors, inside the house, marked with our scent, with the human scent, with the dog scent? Yes, of course it is. Is this door not, then, overkill?

From Out of Doors

Once we have been Out of Doors and patrolled our area, and when we are sure that no Othercats will make this their home for at least the foreseeable future—the foreseeable future being the time it takes for us to return to the inside of the house and be closed in behind the door that is so often closed behind us as if there was some use in closing it other than to be bothersome to us—we remember that we have not been Indoors during all this time that we have been patrolling Out of Doors, and it is possible that someone has eaten our food or is sleeping on our computer monitor or is running water in the bathroom (we are desperately thirsty).

To get the Laps' attention when we are Out of Doors we have two options. We may sit or lie on the table outside the front window, where we may be seen by a passing Lap, but this method is sometimes too subtle for our Laps. (It would be so much easier if

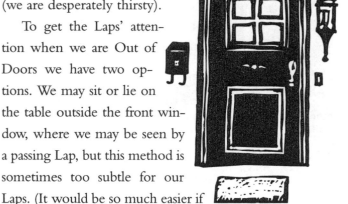

they left it open. Did we say that already? Are we becoming repetitive? Do you sense a theme? We hope so, especially if it will mean removal of the door.) We may also sit at the door and vocalize our complaint until someone comes to the door— *"Wreeow,"* we say, and again *"Wreeow,"* until someone comes to the door (again, why did they bother closing it, knowing what they must about our having been outside and needing to return?). Or, finally, we may combine the two techniques by sitting on the table outside the front window where we may be seen by a passing Lap and we may vocalize our complaint until someone comes to the door and opens it for us to come Indoors.

"Wreeow! Wreeow!"

"Didn't I just let you out?" says Scratch, who has come dangerously close to shutting the door on our tail. "What is this game?" he says.

Sometimes, if we have resorted to this last method, it is very nearly too late. If it takes them too long to open the door for us, we will remember that we spent a lot of time trying to get them to let us in, and it has therefore been an extremely long time since we last visited the telephone pole. So when Scratch stands at the open door and says, "Come inside, you ridiculous cat," we go toward the door, we look inside the door, but then we turn our back on him and walk toward the steps. "What on earth is your deal?" he says, then waits and watches us as we sit near the top of the steps, where the mailman will soon come to deliver the mail, and he closes the door again with a sigh.

Scratch understands territory. It is why he sometimes sits on the front steps with a glass of iced tea and a magazine. As he does so, he is saying, "These are my front steps. This is my iced tea." Mom does the same, but tends to sit at the table, and for a shorter time. She has other places to tend, to mark as her own. Some days she seems to scent-mark the entire house, just as we do.

Now we go to the telephone pole. It is not as satisfying as we thought it would be to climb and scratch and make it freshly ours. We rub and climb and claw. But no matter how much we climb and rub, it continues to have these unusual odors in addition to ours. It almost—almost—doesn't seem worth the trouble.

We return to the front door and begin again.

WINDOW

The window (and by the window we mean the window in the front room behind the sofa, where a cat may lie and look out at the world as it passes by) is nothing but a tease, both from the inside and the outside. We may see all that is happening on the other side of the window, but we may not pass through the window without interference.

We have, at times, attempted to swat at an insect or

other small whirling creature on the other side of the window, but to no avail. *Bat bat bat.*

Nothing.

A tease.

If we could keep ourselves from looking through the window, we would. But there is Movement outside the window. We are incapable of resisting the admiration of movement. We very much would like to be a participant in the activities that occur through the window, and when we are allowed out through a door (*if* we are allowed out through a door), we often wonder what it was we were so enthusiastic about, and we return to the window, to sit on the table just outside the window, to watch the movement inside the house, wanting now to be a participant of that movement.

We understand the Laps sometimes have a similar problem with their own window. They call this win-

dow Television, and through the Television they can watch what happens just there on the other side of the Television window glass, and though they may want to participate, the Television window glass does not allow it. We wonder if there is a door through which the Laps can enter the movement on the other side of the Television window glass. If there is such a door, our Laps have not, so far as we know, passed through it.

Just as with any of the performing arts (dance, theater, rolling in the grass, tree climbing, etc.), watching Movement through the window should be considered its own reward.

LAP HAIR

Though we did not end up suckling on the hair of our Laps, it is not so much because we were unsatisfied with the hair per se, but because whenever we would do so the Lap in question would begin to laugh. "That tickles, Kitty. Ack. Stop it, Kitty." We would then be pushed away or lifted off or otherwise moved from our suckling pose.

But Lap hair has long had an attraction for us, and it is full of Lap scentmarking like no other part of their body.

When possible, we will approach the hair of one of our Laps, especially Fly or Kittengirl, so as to imprint their scentmark on us and so that we may imprint them with our scentmark. (For obvious reasons, it is advisable to always approach Kittengirl when she is sleeping.)

To a large degree, we are responsible for their well-being, and it is best if we are able to share this imprint, so that we may always be able to find one another, even if blinded.

CATFLAP

We may have mentioned our dislike of doors placed in entryways, and to a large extent this remains true no matter how quickly Scratch responds to our request to Open the Door.

Some Laps have found a solution to the problem of the door. They have embedded a second, smaller door in the large door that a cat of our size has no trouble pushing through, either in or out.

The house across the street from our house has such a door, and for a long time there were no humans living in this house, and we made the Indoors of this house a part of our territory. We would sleep in the vacant house on especially cold nights, and we would explore the drifting odors and motes of the empty house.

We enjoyed having this entire house to ourselves, and we would have continued to occupy this territory had the New Laps not suddenly appeared, as we pushed our way through the catflap, and greeted us with "Oh, hello, Kitty. Can we help you with something?"

Worse, the New Laps brought with them an extremely large and unruly spotted dog that gave chase immediately, and we used the cat door one last time to leave this home immediately, never to return. Luckily, this spotted dog was too large to fit through the catflap and follow us, though we see him sometimes in their backyard, and he regularly escapes over the fence, like a cat.

We sometimes approach the house and explore the scentmarkings there (mostly doglike scentmarkings), but we do not enter, even if we are positive that the dog is in the backyard.

But back to our point: Why does our great castle of a home not have a door such as this one? What error of judgment must have caused this architectural flaw?

We have explored other houses in the neighborhood but have found no other doors such as this one. Perhaps this door is but an exception. Or perhaps it is an infant technology, not yet adopted by the majority of Laps. Whatever the reason, we look forward to spreading the word of the cat door. We ask for no less than a cat door in every home where there lives a cat, and a meal ready the moment we are hungry. This does not seem so far out of reach.

Spread the word.

3

INDOORS

A great number of us live our entire lives (or nearly our entire lives) inside our Fortress or Castle or other Residence. That is, we live behind doors, or on the inside of doors, or (to be brief) Indoors. We don't know why this is, exactly, except perhaps that the Laps within require the talents of a Skilled Cat Indoors more than Out of Doors, and the adaptable cat finds this an agreeable arrangement, especially if there is actual work to be done Indoors.

(This is not a predicament we have had to endure, so far, as we are allowed outside often, but a cat never knows, and we sometimes sit patiently beside the door waiting, wondering if we will ever be allowed outside again— if we have, indeed, become one of the cats that lives only Indoors. It has not yet happened to us, thank goodness.)

There is work everywhere, of course, so the adaptable cat never lacks work, even if that work is satisfied Indoors, by just being the cat, the beautiful and mysterious cat of the house.

YARN

The yarn begins in a ball. The yarn is kept in a ball because otherwise it is unruly, all stretched out like yarn can be, all over the place crazy and difficult to manage. How useful is that? It is more useful as a ball because—oh, look at that, how it unrolls and moves and bounces, we swat and the ball unravels—there it goes! Down the stairs! Chase and pounce!

We give chase and swat the ever-unwinding madness of the ball and it unravels as it travels and catches in our paws, and we swat and wrap it around us and we swat again and chase the ball down the stairs and around and through the shoes, into the living room and through the chair legs, until it is no longer in a ball, at which time it becomes unruly again. Just yarn. Yarn yarn yarn. A wild display of color on the carpet. Art, perhaps, if we value art, which we don't. A hazard to the passing cat now. This art is hazard. So we retreat—*zap!*—to the dining room, to the hallway, to the bathroom, to see if the end of the toilet paper roll is within reach.

Is it?

It is!

Vacuum

We don't know what all the fuss is about. (Have you seen how the ridiculous dog reacts to the vacuum?) When the vacuum comes to life (it is obviously a living thing), we simply disappear.

It is best to be outside at this time.

If we have been sleeping when the vacuum awakens, we will first note our displeasure with a glance at whichever Lap woke the vacuum. Then we will disappear.

Mirror

We have seen ourselves, we think. In the hallway and in the bathroom.

One way (the best way) to know whether a cat is Us or Not Us is by scent. We do not need to spend much time examining scent, on sniffing and smelling and discovering the different scents of the cat in question. Not like a dog. We encounter a cat scent long before we encounter the cat. And therefore we know when the cat approaches us, when the cat is within sight, that this cat is not the same cat as us. And we assume that this cat also knows that we are not them.

When a cat is us, it has almost no scent at all. Or rather, we do not exactly smell the cat because it is a scent we carry with us and therefore do not notice. So this cat here must be us.

So far we have only encountered ourselves in the house, either in the hallway near the bathroom door or in the bathroom itself, while standing on the counter. We can almost always find ourselves there, looking back at us. We assume that the us we find there is either always waiting for us to appear, to show us what it is we look like, or that the us there knows when we are coming and appears when necessary. We have never failed to appear when standing in these exact places. We know this cat in this place is us both because of the lack of scent and because our movements are exactly duplicated in the cat we find there. We have never seen a cat that is not us so easily and quickly duplicate our movements.

We do not bristle at our appearance or attempt to communicate. After all, it is just us, and we are hardly a threat to ourselves at all.

We do notice, however, just how lovely we are. Have you noticed how well groomed our fur has been lately? We have been taking special care around our shoulders, which is very difficult (having to turn so very far in reverse to reach our shoulders with our tongue), but which is clearly paying off. See how it lies, how smooth and lustrous?

We wonder, do the Laps have this contraption so they can see us here even when we are somewhere else? Perhaps they do. It would make sense to have such a device. In fact, we wish we had one to carry with us, so that we might look into it after grooming outside the house, to see exactly how nicely we have groomed ourselves.

Then again, after serious grooming we are usually too tired to spend much time admiring ourselves, as we are properly tired now.

Must nap.

THE PIANO

The piano is a tall piece of furniture that sits in the living room. It is a good piece of furniture on which to escape from a Stampede of Dogs or a Herd of Lap Children. We do so daily, hopping first onto the piano bench, then onto the brilliant white teeth of the piano.

The piano is one of the few pieces of furniture in the house that is apparently alive. When we jump onto its teeth, the piano complains with bright, remarkable noise. We do not mind the bright, remarkable noise, but we are often surprised by it, and have to jump quickly to the top of the piano to look back at the teeth in wonder, asking ourselves, "Has it always done that?"

Perhaps it has. We're not quite sure.

We quickly decide it doesn't matter, of course, and regain our composure almost immediately so that we can sit at the edge of the piano, as nonchalant as the situation will allow, utterly ignoring the Stampede of Dogs or Herd of Laps.

Furthermore, we rather enjoy, at times, the complaints of the piano, except that when we step on the teeth it seems to alert both children and dogs (whichever is not currently stampeding or herding) of our presence, and they frequently come to explore what it is that has disturbed the piano. Still, we are out of reach of the dogs, and we are no longer under the feet of the Laps, so it doesn't matter much.

Sometimes another member of the household will also be alerted, and they may chime in with "That's lovely, Kitty. Can you play *The Minute Waltz*?"

This seems to amuse them. So far, their amusement has caused us no harm.

In any case, they know very well how difficult it is to play Chopin without any fingers.

TELEPHONE

When Mom holds the telephone and talks, she is obviously talking to us. There is often no one else in the house, so who else could she be talking to? The dogs? We don't think so. The dogs are either begging for food or they have left the room altogether.

So we approach her. We circle and scentmark her. We wait nearby, on a chair, and look at her. We may talk back, in cat language, and if she is sitting at the table we may put our face in her face, so that we can more appropriately converse. A properly intimate cat conversation can only be had at very close range.

The things she says as she holds the phone appear to be nonsen-sical, as if she is talking to someone not even in the room. This is also common among cats. Shared intimacies may be nonsensical, so we are not surprised. We are surprised, however, at just how feline Mom appears to be. We are glad of this, as it reminds us of our own mother, and it causes us to make the meditation sound the Laps know as *purr*. We meditate as we share this intimacy with Mom.

"Not now, Kitty—no, not you, the cat—she's . . ."

Such beautiful nonsense.

TABLE

As long as there is no food on the table, they do not bother to push us off when we jump up. Even if there is food on the table, though, it is often worthwhile to jump up. It is a good place from which to survey the room or to escape being trampled, and there are many good things to be found on the table.

For instance, there is often a fresh cup of water on the table that one of the Lap children has left there. If there is a fresh cup of water on the table (it tends to be fresher than the water in our water dish, even moments after someone has replenished our water dish—the water in the water dish is simply not as fresh as this water here in the cup, because this smells fresher—more like fresh water), we can either try to drink the water out of the cup with our tongue (a technique that rarely works, as the children often drink some of the water before they leave it for us on the table and our tongue is not long enough to reach the water and our head is not small enough to fit inside the cup), or we can bat at the cup with our paw until it tips over, at which point we can drink from the spilled water (as it escapes across the table, much like a river or even a waterfall) at will, or until Scratch comes into the room shouting, "Cat, dammit, you spilled the water again, didn't you?"

He waves at us with his hand as if to tell us to get down from the table, but we aren't finished drinking, so we do nothing until he picks us up and drops us onto a chair. Then we go to the other side of the table, under a chair, and wait for him to leave. When he does, we jump back onto the table.

"Off!" he says, picking us up again and dropping us to another chair. He has a towel now. He's wiping the water off the table.

We are not as thirsty as we were before, and we wonder how thirsty we actually were in the first place. It's hard to remember after having drunk the water how thirsty we were before having drunk the water.

Perhaps we were not so thirsty, but we drink when there is an opportunity to do so, not when we are thirsty. A cat can never tell when the next drink of water might be the last.

Box

New Box

Like many things in life, an open box is not so much a place in which to put something (though Laps are always trying to put something inside a box, as if that is what it is for) as it is an invitation to sleep. We will accept this invitation. As long as there are no squirrels in the vicinity. If there are squirrels, we will not have time to sleep, but right now we do not see any squirrels.

So we will sleep. And how lovely of the Laps to provide us with this very fine cat bed. It is very much like the one we had in mind.

Except, of course, without the gold filigree. In fact, there is practically no ornamentation on this bed whatsoever. Did they think we would not notice? Perhaps next time they will remember, at the very least, the gold filigree?

No matter. This will do for now. Which reminds us. It must be time for a nap.

Box Recycled

Where is our bed? It used to be here, on the floor, beside the stairs. Did the Laps move it? Are they having it engraved? Will it return with the gold filigree?

Or did the dog carry it off? Is the dog sleeping in it? The dog does tend to sleep in other creatures' beds. It is possible that the dog is sleeping there, though we do not think the dog would fit in the bed without ruining it. We hope the dog did not take it.

But as long as we cannot find the bed where it is supposed to be, we will look outside. We will stand by the door and call to be let outside. Perhaps we will look for the bed, or perhaps we will sleep on the steps, in the sun, where someone might step should someone leave the house. That way we will know when they are attempting to escape.

P A P E R   B A G

What is so fascinating about the paper bag left on the floor?

Honestly, we are not quite sure. But see what happens when we step on the bag. It not only makes noise but also looks as if something might be trapped in the bag, as if there is a mouse or bird in there. Perhaps a wild goat, even.

But when we enter the bag, all we find is darkness. Even in the darkness, though, as we step further into the recesses of the paper bag, we discover that it continues to move as if that animal is in here, as if maybe the bag is a practical joker.

We have spent many hours attempting to discover the secrets of the paper bag, to no avail. Even when we surprise it, leaping from a high place, the paper bag acts exactly the same way, and we find no creature inside. How does that work? By what physical laws does it operate?

It is a mystery. And we do love a good mystery. Just not one at our expense.

COMPUTER

We do not pretend to know what it is you use the computer for. We use it for heat and sleep, obviously, and we suppose it is possible you use it for the same, as we notice that quite often when you are sitting at the computer, you begin to yawn and stretch so terribly that you have to get up and find a more comfortable place for taking a nap. As long as you do not pretend that the computer is more useful to you than it is to us, we are satisfied that its utility is understood to be intrinsic.

Hostage

As long as we stand here and hold this toy hostage (a toy the Laps sometimes call a mouse, though this makes no sense to us at all since it does not resemble any sort of mouse we have ever seen), the Laps will not use the computer. It is ours, this computer. Did we not make that clear when we made this house our domain? You may sit in the chair before the screen, and you may operate the toys that click and tick and tap, but you may not shoo us off the monitor.

This is your last warning. One false move, and the mouse is history.

Keyboard

When we walk across the keyboard, the fish disappear from the computer monitor and we create a message there that looks like this:

Z XvS hgujp [h] ui]; uuu kkk l.
]g[ftrtio vcx 5esA jnbh gsfsc Azsa [::\
d9 q nn vuaght

The message is not so much in what we have typed but in what we mean by having typed. What we mean is that you are not paying adequate attention to us. We need to lie in your lap or rub against some part of you that you recently washed, or we need to groom your sideburns—they are becoming unruly.

K I T C H E N   R U G

We know you are coming. We can feel you, even as we sleep, just as we would feel the approach of a wildebeest, and we wake, ready. When we open our eyes, we sense in your step "going toward the refrigerator" and also "opening the refrigerator," and even "moving cat so as to access refrigerator." But we are here, on the rug in front of the refrigerator, and we would rather not move from this spot. So let us tell you something about this refrigerator. You only *think* you need to open the refrigerator. There is nothing in there for you. There is nothing worth having, except maybe a raw egg in a bowl, or a scoop of the soft fishy food, but you do not have the "feeding the cat" look about you, so we are not moving. We will take some convincing if you really want to get in there.

Furthermore, that refrigerator is in an impossibly ridiculous position very near our food and water, and directly before this perfect rug, upon which we may sleep for many hours (or even minutes or seconds) and stay cool while, at the same time, enjoying the rug's divine viscosity. We must inform you that should you consider moving us from this position, we will be forced to sharpen our claws on the sofa while you attempt to make yourself a sandwich. It's your choice. But we know which we would choose.

S C R A T C H I N G   P O S T

There is a carpeted post in the living room that we understand is meant for us. We are to scratch this post instead of scratching the furniture. But this is quite ridiculous. The purpose of scratching the furniture cannot be replaced by scratching the post. (Though we sometimes scratch the post, we do not do so as a *replacement* for scratching the chair but *in addition* to scratching the chair.) We scratch the chair because the chair is a favored place in the household, and favored places must receive both a scentmark and a physical mark. We scratch the chair because having done so, we mark a favored place as ours as well as yours.

The scratching post? It is only ours. And though it can be used to sharpen claws, and though it is a good idea to indicate that it is ours, it can never replace this chair, and we will continue to scratch and scentmark the chair, as we are so doing this moment.

"Cat!" It is also a good idea to scratch when within

hearing distance of one of the Laps, because we mark this as both ours and theirs as much for their benefit as for ours (they rarely do it themselves). You would think they would be grateful. But Mom is coming at us with the squirt bottle and we have to move quickly. The squirt bottle means we are about to become wet. We have had just about enough of wet.

SQUIRT BOTTLE

The Laps own a squirt bottle full of water that they squirt in our direction to indicate displeasure. The squirt bottle is similar to a squirt gun, and we assume both are toys, used to cheer the user. In general, an adult Lap is in a foul mood when using the squirt bottle, and likely is shouting something like "No!" or "Don't eat the plant!" When they are in such a foul mood, it is a good idea for us to leave the room so as not to become wet by misuse of the squirt bottle. The Laps are reckless in their use of the squirt bottle and when they use it, they may squirt water onto us.

We do not appreciate this recklessness, but Laps do not seem to have complete control of their bodies and often veer off course. We have tried to teach them meditation techniques in order to better control themselves, but they do not often practice.

If they were to practice, they would likely be in such

control of their bodies and their emotions that they would no longer need to use the squirt bottle at all.

H A L L W A Y

We are on alert at the end of the hallway. Some day. Some. Day. Down this passage will come a giant rodent. A rodent so large that we might at first mistake it for some other animal. (Is that a Bison from the plains of South Dakota? A stampeding African Elephant? The return of the great Woolly Mammoth?) But it won't take us long to recognize, and when we do, we will be ready, present, here, waiting. Plotting. Our Plan of Attack. Even if we are asleep, we will be most ready.

Sleeping now. But ready. Woolly Mammoth indeed.

C L O S E T   D O O R

Behind this door? Wonders unknown. We discovered which wonders they were last time the door was opened and we passed through the door, but for some reason we don't remember what the wonders are, so we would appreciate your opening the door so we can remind ourselves.

"Cat," says Mom, "it's a closet." We rub against the door trim and scentmark, then turn and scentmark again, then say, "Prrreow!"

"Okay," she says. "But we did this last week and nothing has changed in there."

She opens the door and we approach the darkness, then look inside. Coats. A vacuum. Some shoes and other assorted items. We sit and peer inside, wondering if this is the same as it was when we looked last time. Probably not. We wander toward a paper bag on the floor and rub against it.

"See?" We look up at Mom. "Just a closet," she says. We blink slowly. Of course it's just a closet. That's exactly what we thought it was. But we needed to be sure of it. And now that we are sure of it, she may close the door.

She closes the door and we scentmark the door and follow her down the hallway. Perhaps she is remembering just now that she has forgotten to put food in our bowl. Though we are not currently hungry, we will follow her to find out. It is always good to know whether there is food in our bowl.

Fewer doors. That's what this house needs. In fact, no doors at all. Then there would be no secrets hidden behind doors. And we could truly make this house our own.

THROUGH THE SCREEN DOOR

Ah, there is the world again. We really should go out there just to be sure the world remembers that it is ours.

If we could just convince the world that these doors are senseless. Useless. Troublesome. Especially these with windows we can see through when standing on our hind legs. What is their purpose except to drive us mad with desire?

See there? A cat passing near our home. And a dog being walked on a lead. Several birds. Hundreds of them. Birds cat bird bird dog bird moth cat bird. Let. Us. Out.

AT THE WINDOW

If it weren't for the glass in this window, we are quite sure the birds would nest inside our home. If this were to happen? Oh, wonders. We dare not think of it.

Also, there are insects inside the house quite often flying against the window, trying to get out, unaware, perhaps, that they will never escape this way (insects have No Brain at All). The movement of the insects is Very Attractive, and we bat at them. It is a kind of practice to bat at the insects here at the window, but it is also rather tedious. The insects are somewhat fragile, and eventually they stop moving. They also have very little meat on them, and are not good-tasting at all.

We are quite sure that if the Laps were to remove the glass in this window, the insects would be very happy to fly away, never to return to the house, and because we know the Laps are not fond of insects, we wonder again at the utility of the glass.

AIR CONDITIONER

Somewhere in this air conditioner there is a family of birds. We can sit on the counter and examine the air conditioner up close, and we do this often. We have examined the air conditioner in the window from both inside the house and outside the house. The birds seem to enter and exit in the gap just below the air conditioner. A great deal of our waking hours is spent watching for and listening to the family of birds as they build and squabble and twitter and feed. We sit on the counter and watch and listen and sometimes move our weight back and forth on our feet, as if readying to pounce. But they do not appear very often, and we see no way to climb the outside wall to get to them. Usually only an adult appears, though we hear baby birds as well. They fly too high and fast for us to catch. So we do not move from our position. We do not want to be spotted.

The birds never appear at all inside the house, but they are much noisier from in here. We are not so careful of being spotted from in here, but look for some way to get in or through the air conditioner.

"You're never going to catch those birds that way," says Scratch.

We ignore him. He obviously does not understand birds, nor the concept of stalking them. We do not necessarily stalk them to catch them. We stalk them, of course, because they are birds.

Stairs

At the Top

It is especially lovely for our home to have such a perfectly shaped space at such a high altitude for us to nap on. Now if we could only prevent Laps from going up and down, we might be able to put together enough solitude for a decent nap. They seem to believe they have business either at the top of the stairs or at the bottom of the stairs. Perhaps it is true that there are preparations to be made for the time that we are awake, but how much work could it be, refilling the food and water bowls to appropriate levels? This is all we ask upon waking.

So please, if you must go up or down the stairs, be mindful of us. Tiptoe, if you can. Or fly. We know that you are burdened with size, but to use a tired metaphor, try to be as quiet as a mouse.

Of course, at the top of the stairs, it may be the mouse we are waiting for, to shimmer past at the bottom of the stairs. We therefore suggest you be even quieter than the mouse so that you do not become our accidental prey.

At the Bottom

At the very bottom of the lowest set of stairs is a large, doorless room that remains cool in the summertime and warm in the wintertime. This room is somehow buffered from the regular variance of temperature outside the house. Since there are no doors in this large space (called a basement, we think), there are many things to explore without interference. Broken furniture, old blankets, laundry full of glorious odors, crumpled papers, dead insects, defunct spiderwebs, Styrofoam packing materials, loose marbles, and small objects of unknown origin. We often sleep on the dirty laundry, as it seems to produce its own good odors and warmth.

We fully expect to find a rodent or other prey in the basement some day. And we will continue to submit our requests for turning the rest of the house into one very large room, top to bottom, just like the basement. In, out, through, the house one giant room.

We sometimes forget, however, that there is one door at the top of the basement stairs that leads into and out of the basement. This door is sometimes shut when we want to leave the basement, and if it is we are not able to make our exit. The longest we have been stuck down here is a full day. There was plenty to do in the basement while we were trapped, of course. But all the while we very much wanted to go up and patrol our territory.

It is a good thing our hearing is so acute. At the slightest sound of the opening door, we were able to dash up the stairs and through the opening door before the opening was much more than a crack.

"Oh, hello, Kitty," said Scratch. "Were you stuck in the basement?"

Such irony in his voice. Is that really necessary?

IN THE SINK

We do not understand or appreciate your fascination with our occupation of the sink portion of the household. The reasons we are here, in the sink—despite the risk of wetness—are obvious, are they not?

The sink is cooler than most places in the house. The coolness from the sink surrounds us as no other coolness can surround us. If there was a sink Out of Doors, that would be one less reason for us to come home at night. But there isn't a sink Out of Doors. So here we are. In the sink. Trying to sleep. Just a nap, you know.

And there you go. Taking our picture again. For publication, we hope. Or perhaps this year's Christmas card?

TOILET PAPER

Toilet paper can be Very Useful to Cats, especially when we are Trapped in the Bathroom or Left Alone Indoors when we want to be Out of Doors.

Sometimes a roll is left out for us (usually on the counter or near the stairs), and other times it is placed in the bathroom, hung from the wall. If it is hung from the wall, we can spend the better part of an hour pulling the paper down, slowly, then quickly, then taking our time to admire the pile of paper, shredding it, pawing at it. There appears to be a never-ending supply of toilet paper collected on the toilet-paper roll. We have never run out of toilet paper after first discovering a roll there. This may be because we become so infatuated with the toilet paper on the floor, in shredding that paper to smallish, movable, pounceable bits, that we lose interest in the roll itself.

When a roll is left out for us, we may use it as a pillow. Or, sometimes, when the mood strikes us, we may bat at it and it will roll away to the great pleasure of our pounce, our chase and jump and stand and pounce.

Small shredded bits of toilet paper everywhere. Truly this is a castle. We make of it whatever we like.

4

OUT OF DOORS

Some of us are allowed Out of Doors. The Out of Doors is sometimes called the Great Out of Doors by Laps who do not know any better (or by Cats Not Allowed Out of Doors). Out of Doors is the usual state of being for a cat, as cats began Out of Doors (we did not invent doors), and had we not adopted Laps as appropriate companions, we would likely have remained Out of Doors creatures. We are obviously, therefore, more familiar with what Out of Doors means than any Lap, and we therefore proclaim that though Out of Doors has its advantages (including the presence of birds and moths, the items of the air, and mice and rabbits, the items of the earth), the Greatness of the Out of Doors is equaled (and sometimes exceeded) by the Greatness of the Indoors, where food is not Chased and Killed but simply Eaten, and where water is not drunk from the ends of grass or from a muddy puddle or an Out of Doors dog bowl but from a tipped-over glass or a just-used bathtub or a running faucet. Out of Doors is Good. Sometimes Great. But if we had to give up one or the other? You likely can guess how we would answer.

FENCE

The backyard fence is extremely useful. When we sit upon the backyard fence, we can survey the area and know precisely when danger approaches. Or, indeed, when prey is nearby.

Furthermore, the fence is an excellent means of escape when another creature is giving chase. Many animals who might chase us are unable to jump upon the fence as we do. From the top of the fence we can make ourselves large and indicate our displeasure, after which we may return to our preferred state of indifference.

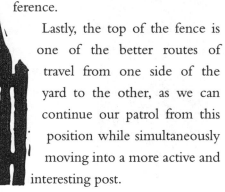

Lastly, the top of the fence is one of the better routes of travel from one side of the yard to the other, as we can continue our patrol from this position while simultaneously moving into a more active and interesting post.

We must note, however, that fences surrounding other yards can be as much nuisance as assistance, especially when such a yard is patrolled by an Othercat, as the yard will likely be well patrolled if it becomes necessary for us to enter that yard, and we are likely to be rebuffed. We are not fond of being rebuffed for any reason, especially by an Othercat who has the advantage of already sitting atop a fence.

There must be something of Great Importance (such as a wild boar or a baby giraffe) on the other side of this fence for us to take on a patrolling Othercat. In general, we have found it is not worth the effort, even for a brightly colored finch.

Automobile

The automobile is a beast of burden, and it carries the Laps from our home to other places in our surroundings, much as a Lap might ride a horse or a camel (we have not seen a Lap riding camelback recently, but we are certain they have done it at some point . . . perhaps it is something we observed on the

Television). Though in general we are not in favor of owning or keeping automobiles for ourselves (there are frankly much better means of travel, such as running, walking, or even slinking), they do have a few purposes for which we are generally grateful.

Hood

When a car has recently pulled into the driveway or has been sitting out in the sun most of the day, the front portion of the car (which is generally broad and flat) can be quite warm enough for a decent nap. There are times when we would like to be Indoors for a nap, but the doors of the house have been closed so we cannot enter the house and we are too tired to make enough of a commotion to get the attention of a Lap.

Often when we sleep on the automobile, if we are approached by someone wanting to use the automobile, they will first warn us.

"You'd better move off, Kitty. Oh, look. Footprints. Could you not wipe your feet first?"

This is Scratch. His sense of humor is what the Laps call "dry." We tend to think of it as "not funny."

There is then just enough time for approximately twenty-three more seconds of our nap before Scratch opens the door and climbs inside to begin the process of bringing the automobile to life. Before the automobile comes to life (usually soon after he shuts the door) we flee toward the front of the house, to sit on the steps and watch him nonchalantly, as if this is where we had been all along. We are always a little surprised that any creature or machine could make such a commotion upon coming to life. Perhaps this is the automobile's complaint at having been woken up. If we were capable of making such a noise upon having been woken up, we would surely do so. We would likely do so right now, especially as there is nobody inside the house who might open the door for us.

We will finish our nap here, on the steps.

Under

We sometimes crouch beneath the automobile, just behind one of the tires, so that we can observe the world without being observed in return. We know enough about our own appearance to know that we are well hidden and well protected from this vantage point. Most prey will not notice us. They are not good with detail. They will notice the car only. Even if it is dusk and our eyes are shining from below the car, the prey will assume that the bright shining objects below the car are part of the car, much as they assume that the quivering tail in the grass is nothing but more tall grass. Prey could notice such things if they took the time, but they prefer to spend their time eating and running away. Some of our prey are quite voracious eaters, but they are also quite fast. That they do not spend enough time observing and understanding the world around them is one of the reasons it does not bother our conscience to hunt and kill them.

Thinking Creatures: An Interlude

In general, cats do not prey on any of the carnivorous creatures not because we feel ourselves in danger but because carnivorous creatures are generally thinking sorts of animals and make a contribution to the earth, unlike unthinking prey, whose contribution to the earth is as Prey to Thinking Creatures.

We are meant to hunt and kill prey. It is what our bodies and minds and claws and eyes are designed to do. And we will use whatever simple means we have at our disposal to make the process of hunting and killing prey easier. In this case, that means hiding beneath the automobile.

Language

We might further note that we do not speak the automobile's language, but we do not believe that it is prey and therefore we do not hunt it. There may be an odd cat here or there that hunts automobiles (and we have seen them chased by dogs and boats), but because the automobile spends a great deal of its day sleeping—even more than most cats—it is likely a predator (of what we do not know, though we are certain most automobiles do not eat cats). Perhaps because the Laps keep the automobile and seem to care for it (almost as much, it seems, as they care for the dog), they may indeed feed it as they feed us. In fact, now that we think about it, we have never seen the automobile hunting or eating, so the Laps must feed it when they take it out with them. Perhaps when we are sleeping.

What Were We Talking About?

Oh yes. Beneath the automobile. Us. Hunting.

Of course, there are times when someone will use the automobile while we are beneath it, and because we are hunting, we might not notice the Lap approach and enter and slam the door, or notice when they've seen us and warned us to move away, and we do not really break from our reverie until the automobile has woken, at which time we will flee and again sit on the steps and watch as the car begins to move. From beneath the automobile, the noise is even more deafening, especially to a cat listening carefully for the sound of rustling nuthatches in the brush. Our heart will only settle down to its normal rate after the automobile has wandered off into the distance and we can no longer hear its roar.

We are hungry and there is nobody here to let us into the house.

What were we hunting again?

We will go to the back door and see if they have left it open for us. Or if they have removed it altogether.

Our hope that the door has been removed is evidence that we are forever optimists, despite all appearances otherwise.

GLOAMING

Gloaming is the time of day between the Day and the Night. It is sometimes called Dusk, though we feel Gloaming is more precise, as it describes all the time at which a cat can best see the creatures that move about in the Out of Doors. That is, we see better than most creatures during the Gloaming moments, and we believe that some creatures are even blinded by the Gloaming, as if perhaps the slice of light offered between Day and Night is designed almost exclusively for cats. Perhaps it was invented by cats. We do not remember. But we believe there has been a Gloaming for as long as there has been a Day and a Night. We therefore feel that the Gloaming was created by the mating of Day and Night. And because it is so designed as the time for cats, we are certain that cats are the favored creatures of both Day and Night, and they gave us this advantage, creating the Gloaming for us, so that we would survive longer than many of the nonsurviving species.

Therefore there are times, just past the Gloaming, when we sit on the steps near the house with our eyes half shut and thank the Day and the Night, the Night and the Day. A creature so honored should always say thank you.

NIGHT

Night is the time of day that is not Day, but is Night. It is also the time of day that is dark.

Calling

At Night, we are hunting for whatever moves in the Night. We can see better than some of the Night creatures, but really we are at our best at the time of day known as the Gloaming (see above).

If we are outside during the Night, at some point Scratch will come to the door and call for us. "Here, Kitty Kitty Kitty Kitty. Come on, Puss. Here, Kitty Kitty Kit. Kit-Kit-Kit-Kit-Kit-Kit-Kit. Come on, Cat. Where are you?"

We know this means we are to come inside, that we are about to miss our last opportunity to come Indoors for the night, but we are unable to move at the moment, tracking the motion of a rabbit near the neighbor's hedge.

"Kitty-Kitty Kitty-Kitty Kitty-Kitty Kitty-Kitty."

Does the neighbor know about this rabbit? We will solve this nuisance for the neighbor. Rabbits are known to be incapable of being a benefit to the earth except as prey, as they are not particularly intelligent (but manage to survive by multiplying rapidly and by being almost half as cute as a very homely cat), so we will take care of this one.

"Kiiiiitty—where are you?"

The rabbit moves. We are tracking it now. Moving ever so slightly toward the rabbit while it is turned away from us. A brown rabbit difficult to see, its motion away from us slowly, slowly moving away.

"Here, Kit-Kit-Kit-Kit-Kit-Kit-Kit."

Scratch is persistent. Good for him. We are glad for this, because he may be just persistent enough to give us time to catch the rabbit and bring it Indoors as an evening offering to the household. Perhaps for tomorrow evening's meal. Hasenpfeffer. When was the last time Scratch made hasenpfeffer?

But his persistence may also spook the rabbit. *Please do not spook the rabbit.*

The rabbit seems to hear something.

Scratch says it louder now. "Here, Kit-Kit-Kit-Kit-Kit-Kit-Kit." We can tell by the way the rabbit's ears move that he hears Scratch calling. The rabbit is getting ready to bolt, to run away. The rabbit has frozen, does not move or breathe, except for the slightest twitch of his nose, his ears. The rabbit believes that if he does not move, he is invisible. Stupid rabbit. Of course we can see him. Sort of.

"Where on earth are you? Come on, Kitty. Come in the house. Kitty-Kitty Kitty-Kitty Kitty-Kitty Kitty-Kitty."

No. The rabbit has bolted, and we are chasing it, but we will not catch it, and even though we know we will not catch it, we cannot keep ourselves from chasing it. We were too far from the rabbit when it bolted—and the rabbit was too close to the hedge—and now it is gone beyond the hedge, somewhere into the yard behind, through another hedge we suppose, into some open space.

We stop.

"Your loss, Cat."

We turn back toward the sound of the door closing on us, closing against us, without us Indoors.

And now we are Out of Doors for the night. We have missed our last opportunity to return to the house.

It is not so bad this way, really.

We lie in the grass for now. The grass is cool and we can wait for the return of the rabbit, should it decide to return. It just might return. If we are patient. If we can wait.

The grass is so cool and lovely. We are good at this. At making the best of the situation presented to us.

We will wait.

Oh no. The neighbor dog is loose. The unruly spotted dog. He has escaped from his yard again.

We are up and over the fence and standing on the picnic table, back arched, hissing at the neighbor dog as he barks at us. There is nothing to fear from the neighbor dog. He is incredibly stupid. But we must let him know we do not appreciate this interruption. We scold him again. He obviously will not remember our scolding. But he must be warned, and we bat at him and hiss some more. A dog can make noise for months at a time without pause.

If we do not warn him against this, he will continue to make the noise, and we will never catch that rabbit.

So much for the homemade hasenpfeffer.

Escape

There are times, at night, when Scratch goes to the door to call us in and we do not come and we do not come, so he closes the door and goes into the kitchen and has a glass of milk. Then, on his way back to the stairs, to go up and lie down to sleep, he tries one more time at the door.

The moment he opens the door? We run out past him, escaping into the night.

"Hey!" he says. "I didn't know you were in here."

He waits a few moments to see if we will come back inside. We will not.

"Darn it," he says. And he closes the door.

Did we want to spend the night outside?

We suppose it is too late to wonder now.

UTILITY POLE

In front of the house is a pole that stands straight up from the ground as if a tree had been planted there in the sidewalk, then stripped of branches once it had reached a sufficient height. This pole has many scents on it, not least of which is the scent of the pole itself. We have approached many poles like this one, and no matter how many times it has been scentmarked, it always primarily smells like this pole. So we scratch at the pole, to leave a visible mark of our territory. We will scentmark it as well, to be sure, but it is best in situations like this one to also leave some physical trace of our presence, of our territory.

The visible marks we leave are relatively small (compared to the marks we sometimes leave on Scratch's arm when we have had enough of his tomfoolery), but they are visible and will do for now. We will have the opportunity to leave fresh marks when we return to the Out of Doors.

TREE

In the neighbor's yard there is a tree that captivates us. Not only does a squirrel live in this tree but also there is a great deal of movement in the tree that may or may not be creature-created (it is somewhat difficult to know without actually climbing into the tree what movement is created by creatures and what movement is created by Unknown Forces). Indeed, rather than being captivated by the tree, the tree sometimes *holds us captive.* For when we climb up into the tree to see what it is that causes the leaves to move as they do (leaf motion is almost as irresistible as squirrel motion), we have some difficulty understanding how it is a cat is supposed to get down again without jumping. So sometimes we stay in the tree until somebody comes to help us. Other times we are forced to jump.

It is not a particularly long jump, as record jumps go, but it is long enough that we would rather have the assistance of one of our Laps.

We look forward to this tree losing its leaves every autumn. When the tree is bare, there is less motion in the tree and it is possible to resist.

In the Grass

Grass has many purposes besides being good for nibbling.

The first purpose of grass is to hide us. Especially tall grass works best, which is one reason we do not appreciate Scratch mowing the lawn. He usually complies by not mowing the lawn, but once in a while he does it, and we are annoyed.

We may attack from the grass. A Pacific Pocket Mouse. A Riparian Brush Rabbit. A leaf that we were quite certain was a Western Snowy Plover.

When we are well hidden in the grass, we may stalk many minutes. Even hours. Our prey (perhaps a Northern Idaho Ground Squirrel or a Black-footed Ferret) is oblivious to our approach, and we may come within a few feet of the prey before pouncing.

Another purpose of grass is for comfort. The grass is cool, especially in the morning. It may be moist, but cool sometimes trumps moist. A shady bit of grass on a hot summer day is like a square of paradise.

The third purpose of grass is for play. There are often insects or bits of fluff and dust and what all in the grass. And if those bits of fluff and dust and what all move (as they often do when disturbed by passing Laps or Dogs or Other Non-Prey Creatures), we pounce, we toss, we roll and attack and allow the kitten just beneath our cat facade to surface. Perhaps a bird or a rabbit will come later. Now there is the fluff and the dandelion seed.

The fourth purpose of grass is just *now.* While we try to remember the fourth purpose, the final item that makes grass so very useful, we will chew on this bit of green. And swallow. And *purr.*

WALKIES

When Mom or Scratch takes the dogs out for a walk (usually it is Mom, as Scratch appears to be the more sedentary of the two adult Laps), this is the perfect opportunity for us to explore beyond our territory. Even better if Fly and Kittengirl come along. If all of them are out and about, they pay little attention to us, and we may follow without being noticed and bothered.

Or at least without being noticed and bothered right away.

Our favorite walk is to the park because the park is so full of wonderful and varied scentmarkings, of dogs and cats and children and birds and hundreds of types of creatures. (Is that the scent of a Pygmy Rabbit? Or is it a Tipton Kangaroo Rat?) Some of the scents are quite fresh, and some seem as old as the park itself.

There are also innumerable trees, and we scratch and mark the trees over marks that were left just sometime today. The trees are like a canopy of shade over us, and on hot summer days the park is more glorious than any place we can imagine—even the spot on Kittengirl's pillow where she rests her head at night and where we often sleep during the day, though this remains a very close second.

We do not approach our Laps too closely so as not to make them overtly aware of our presence. We have been spotted, to be sure, but they are leaving us alone, for now. We circle the perimeter of their play. The children are climbing upon play structures, the dogs are chasing balls, and we are overcome with the sense that the world is much larger than we had imagined. We wonder if it doesn't get larger each time we go Out of Doors. Larger each time we follow our Laps to the park.

We feel small, but important nonetheless. Our Laps are watching out for us. We sense their attention.

We sometimes wonder if we dare come back here without our Laps. It is not so far off, after all. It is within quick walking distance.

But then we doubt that it will be necessary. The draw of our home is tremendous, and only when taking the inhabitants of our home with us do we care to be away. Pick us up and set us down miles from here, and we will be drawn to our home. We track our home always as we track the children and other creatures. We always have a sense for where it is.

We mark another tree. And when we are finished, we turn to find our Laps disappeared.

Were they abducted?

Did they leave us alone on purpose?

Is this a joke?

If so, it is not a funny joke.

Something might happen to them, and if it happens to them while they are out of our sight, then not only will we be responsible for whatever happens, we will also be without them.

If something is going to happen to them, we would like it to happen to us as well.

But now we are not being especially catlike, for we are worrying about probabilities that are so minuscule as to be nonexistent.

And anyway, when they have gone, the draw of our home is so strong that it seems out of our control. We must return home immediately. And on our way toward home, just a few steps onto the sidewalk that will take us home, we spot them, the dogs and children pulling Mom in four directions at once. This is gratifying to see. So full of unexpected and unexplored magic.

There's magic in the earth when we touch it with our feet. Do you feel it too?

5

HEALTH AND HYGIENE

We are, in general, the cleanest of creatures, because it is in our nature to groom ourselves approximately 80 to 90 percent of our waking hours (as we understand percentages). Even if we wanted to not groom, to let our fur go without grooming, we wouldn't be able to do it. You might say to us, "Have you tried to stop grooming?" And we would reply, "We cannot try. It is not in our nature to try. And furthermore, what would this accomplish?" And you might say, "You could be doing something more important in the time you normally spent grooming." And we would reply, "We do not know of anything more important than grooming, and we have not been presented with any activity more important than grooming, and we doubt any Lap or other creature could present us with such an activity. Should some activity present itself, we will take up that activity, but our involvement in said activity will likely be short-lived, and presently you will find us again grooming."

We recommend regular grooming (even for Laps and other creatures such as dogs and llamas and chimpanzees, who we understand groom, but incompletely). The old saying (we do not know the source, though it was likely a Wise Creature) is quite true: Cleanliness is next to Catliness.

GROOMING

Grooming is a necessity as much as sleeping or eating or drinking water or mating (though the necessity of mating could easily be argued against) or sleeping. We must groom for our survival. Beyond the necessity of cleaning the blood from our kill off our bodies (if we do not clean the blood, our prey will smell us coming for many miles—they may not be intelligent, but they have an acute sense of smell), we also groom so that our fur does not become matted and ugly. Should our fur become matted and ugly, our abilities as workers, as royalty, as Creatures of Great Stature, will be damaged, and we may lose our position in the Great Parade of Earthly Creatures. We may lose our food source. We may lose rights to the big puffy chair.

We shudder at the thought.

Simply shudder.

Then we go to the big puffy chair and sharpen our claws, leave our scentmark, and climb up to the seat, where a Lap would sit if a Lap were present, and we groom ourselves, all the time thinking, "We will not lose our rights to the big puffy chair. We will not."

M U T U A L   G R O O M I N G
A N D   P E T T I N G

Many creatures have helpmates when it comes to grooming. They may pair up with another creature of their species. Or they may groom as a family unit. The cat is one of the few species so adaptable as to accept grooming from another species.

Humans

Laps call it *petting,* but it is really just a misunderstood form of grooming. If we are in the mood for grooming, we will allow it, as long as the Laps are grooming a part of us that requires grooming—a part of us that feels as if it needs to be groomed, or petted (as it were).

Even if we do allow petting, we only allow it for so long, as determined by an internal cat clock that regulates the amount of time allowed for grooming (and the amount of time allowed for everything else, for that matter). Laps have a difficult time understanding how long this amount of time is, and sometimes we have to let them know with a swat or a bite (depending on how persistent they are) so that they will stop.

When they are finished, we will need to groom ourselves. We will need to remove as much of the Lap scent from us as possible so as not to be mistaken for a Lap. We do not know what sort of predator endangers a Lap, but it would be foolish to leave Lap scent on our bodies just so we could find out.

When we have finished removing the scent from our fur, it may again be time for the parts of us that we cannot reach with our tongue (such as the area behind our ears and neck) to be groomed again by our Laps. If so, we may return to the Lap for petting. If the Lap is an enthusiastic sort, it may pet us again.

Others

So long as the creature is from our Catfamily, we will allow a certain amount of mutual grooming. Sometimes we may be groomed by another cat, by a Lap, by a dog, or even by a raccoon (don't ask—it's a bit of an embarrassment to us—but if a raccoon is a member of our Lap family, well, you can imagine we have little choice but to accept it, being the good-natured creature we are). We may return this grooming as long as it is desired (not all species appreciate the necessity of mutual grooming). Even a Lap will accept grooming if it is presented properly.

H A I R B A L L S

We are aware that our grooming practice sometimes causes the hair we consume in the process to become blocked in our stomach, and it may exit from our mouth, usually in the middle of the night, near the front door (that we wish we could open so we could avoid the unpleasantness of leaving not just a hairball but also the scent of our weakness so near the front door), and the door is near the bottom of the stairs, which is actually a good place to leave the hairball because Scratch is likely to step on or near it in the morning, and will both clean up the hair and mask the scent with orange-scented solution.

The knowledge of where the hairballs come from is not enough to cause us to stop the practice of grooming, however. No matter how uncomfortable and disgusting the hairball, the grooming is so much more important. Can you imagine how uncatlike we would be with matted hair? With the blood of our prey on our paws? Smelling of Laps and dogs and whatever creatures have passed on the lawn the night before?

We will continue to groom as necessary, and we resign ourselves to the knowledge that hairballs happen.

LITTER BOX

Yes, we will use the litter box if necessary, but we prefer to find a remote area of outdoor wilderness, somewhere outside our domain but close enough that we do not have to cross into some Othercat's domain. We cover and hide what we have done so as not to alert prey to our presence.

We suppose that given some cats' need to remain and work Indoors, the litter box is necessary, and the need to hide odor from prey is reduced. There is very little prey Indoors (other than Flies, Moths, and the occasional dust mote). And when trapped Indoors ourselves, we will reluctantly use the litter box as a last resort, as long as some Lap agrees that the litter box must be changed upon occasion. If the litter box is not changed upon occasion, we reserve the right to pee in the bathtub.

DOG MESS

When one of the dogs makes a mess on the floor, it apparently expects us to cover it up; the dog tends to leave the mess and walk away, as if the mess could cover its own odor. We have, at times, attempted to cover the odor by swiping at the floor nearby, but the floor is especially difficult to dig up, and it is nearly impossible to mask the odor.

We have suggested to the dogs that if they need to, they could use the litter box, but when the time comes they seem to forget about the litter box. We do not really blame them for this, as we often forget about the litter box ourselves and would love nothing more than to have immediate and frequent access to Out of Doors. This would simplify matters for both us and the dogs.

We suggest Laps simply remove the doors. They are nothing but an annoyance, really, and cause more trouble than they are worth.

We hope you will take this into consideration. A street full of houses without doors would be a kind of cat paradise. How glorious.

T H E   S H O W E R

Once Scratch tried to take us with him into the shower. This was unwise. We did not like this. The shower, as many creatures know (especially cats), is wet. We do not like wet. Why Scratch would take us into the shower we do not know. We were still a kitten when he took us into the shower, so we do not remember precisely his reasoning, but it may have had something to do with catnip. If there is a human equivalent to catnip, his actions may have had something to do with an overconsumption of it. He must have been intoxicated.

We were unable to get a good hold on his arm, though we dug our claws into his skin as far as they would go. And when he brought us closer, we jumped toward his body, though he still had a hold on us, and eventually we were allowed to go free, scrabbling wildly on the slippery bathroom linoleum.

When we had calmed ourselves (it took only a few moments, really), we sat near the shower and licked our wet paws, waiting for Scratch to remove himself from the shower. When he did, we ran from him, thinking him ready to do whatever it was he just did a second time.

As kittens, we are sometimes forgetful.

Why are we wet?

JUMPER

A healthy cat is a jumping cat. We practice jumping, Indoors and Out of Doors. We jump to catch birds, to escape those who might chase us (dogs, of course, or stampeding elephants). Inside we have jumped to the top of the refrigerator and the bookcase. Out of Doors we have found several trees with branches just high enough to practice our jumping. We may also jump up and scratch the trunk of a tree to show just exactly how powerful a jumper we are to any passing Othercats.

We have sometimes noticed that once we have jumped up to where we are able to jump, it is problematic to jump down again. Jumping down is a skill that we have, but everyone knows that the distance down from a place is much greater than the distance up. Therefore, if you could come and help us down from the bookshelf, that would be excellent.

VETERINARIAN

We do not like the automobile for precisely the reason that the automobile leads directly to the animal hospital. We are at the animal hospital, and we are not pleased. We are in a smallish cage and we would rather be stuck in the walls of the house (again) than be here. We use our voice— *"Wreeooooolw"*—to tell Scratch that we are not happy to be here.

It is further disconcerting to be here, of course, because we were forced to travel not only in the cage (or crate, as they call it, but this is more to assuage their guilt than to describe what it actually is) but also in the company of the two dogs. Why are we traveling with the two dogs?

Scratch is talking to the people who operate the animal hospital. He is trying to control the larger of the two dogs, the black and overwhelming one we used to mistake for our mother (we were very young—we don't make this mistake anymore). She is pulling away from him quite successfully. If anything, she is more concerned about being here than we are.

The second, crazy, manic, out-of-control dog is frantically pacing at the end of her lead, approaching every person and creature in the room (and even some inanimate objects), trying to determine what on earth is going on.

Scratch says, "I'm not sure bringing 'em in all at once is worth saving the ten percent."

The woman he's talking to laughs politely. She is not actually amused. She is busy with some other feature of her job.

In a few moments we are in another room, on a metal table, and the Veterinarian (this is not a word we can say, even to ourselves, even in our head, not because it is too difficult but because it nauseates us) and her assistant hold us, prod us, look around and inside us, measuring and— oh! *That was certainly impolite.*

Then a sharp pain on our hindquarters. A kind of warm moving feeling there, and cold at the same time. Warm and cold and moving.

And then it is over and they return us to the crate. We were first. It is over. This is how we prefer it.

But later, Scratch is going to get a talking to about bringing us here. We weren't even ill. This visit serves no purpose except to satisfy whatever requirements are dictated by societal norms. We will have to look into those requirements and see if we can't arrange to have them changed.

COLLAR

We understand that the collar you place on us means something to you. We understand that you find it beautiful. We know that we are beautiful when wearing the collar. We understand too that the bell attached to the collar makes a lovely noise, and that the lovely noise informs you of our presence and makes you happy to know that we are nearby, that we are approaching, maybe about to enter the house and have our ears scratched (just there behind our ears, thank you). But what we don't understand is the magical properties with which it is endowed.

Let us explain.

Before the new jingly collar? We were able to catch two, maybe three birds a day. But now, even when we use great stealth, and when we perform our most successful bird-swatting move, we are always unsuccessful. And we think it must have something to do with the collar, because the change was almost immediate.

It is beyond our capability to remove the collar. So we must ask you if you know of any antihunting voodoo that has been placed on it. Is it a normal collar, or has it been hexed? Should we be worried that it has other powers we have not yet discovered?

We do not think of it often, but when we do think of it, we are very concerned. If this continues, will you remove it for us? Please?

INJURY

Once we did, indeed, need the (shudder) Veterinarian. We didn't think (at the time) that we needed her, but we suppose it was (in the end) a good thing that we went.

It was a fight, you see. Not a long or life-threatening fight. Not worth mentioning, really, except for the rather painful tear made by our opponent in our hindquarters (which we guard carefully to this day).

We had it taken care of, to a degree. We hid it well. It

is always a good idea, when injured, to act as if uninjured, to go about business as if nothing at all has happened. This keeps enemies from returning to take us on in a weakened state (though we are never truly weak—you understand our meaning).

It was several days before anybody noticed what had happened. We licked our wound in private, out of sight. We spent a great deal of time in the bedroom where honored guests sleep. But after those several days we were not feeling our best. We did not move quickly, and we spent very little time Out of Doors. We had trouble jumping up to the counter to eat our food. And that is when Scratch noticed our injury.

"Oh no," he said. "Looks like you did get nicked in that fight."

Mom came to examine us with him, and they decided to take us to the animal hospital.

Honestly, we don't remember much about our visit there, or the time following. What we do remember is the collar they made us wear that prevented us from seeing even half of what we are accustomed to seeing and prevented us from licking our wound (infuriating, really, because if we can't lick the wound it will likely just take longer to heal). We were sleepy all the time. Even when we would normally have been Out of Doors hunting and Very Active, we were sleepy. We slept. We were confined to a larger crate that smelled very strongly of dog. We were forced to use a litter box (incomprehensible), and ate and drank in the crate (incomprehensible), until several days later we were finally allowed out of the crate for a few hours at a time and allowed to remove our hideous collar and move about.

We had to admit that we were feeling a little better, but also a little dizzy.

It took us a while to realize that our tired dizziness usually followed the time Scratch brought us a small morsel of food and an unusual liquid to drink from a tube. We think, perhaps, that he might have unwittingly been giving us the wrong medication. Something that made us sleep too much.

In any case, it turned out fine in the end. We hardly ever think of it anymore. Except when they put us in the crate and deliver us to the Veterinarian. Incomprehensible. No need for it. Do they believe these visits will keep us from fighting other cats?

Are they so stupid as that?

6

FRIENDS AND RELATIONS

Ours is a difficult, if not impossible, task. Imagine for a moment that you are a cat and living your life knowing exactly how much you are loved. Imagine the responsibility of such knowledge. A burden for us, it very well is.

Admittedly, it is a burden we bring upon ourselves. It is obviously not possible for Laps to love us any less than they do. We are, as you may know, irresistible.

LOVING KITTENGIRL

If we do not run from her, Kittengirl may try to lift us into the air and hold us in a way that causes us a great deal of discomfort. If she tries to lift us up, she most likely will do it awkwardly, and we may have to let out a "Yeowl," which is a request for her not to do what it is she is doing. She does not appear to understand this. If her parents are nearby, they may also let out a kind of yeowl, which sounds more like this: "Careful, honey. Put the cat down, please. No, that means she wants you to put her down, sweetie." Kittengirl does not necessarily listen to her parents any more than she listens to us. In this, as in many ways, she is just like a kitten.

We do not want to hurt Kittengirl, so we do not scratch at her or bite her. Eventually, she understands that we are really too heavy for her to carry far, especially when we are moving about, trying to shake ourselves free of her grip. She will drop us then. But she has to discover this on her own.

In this way, Kittengirl is both very much like us (she has to discover things on her own) and very like a kitten (she does not listen as carefully as she could). This is another of the reasons why we run from her, but it is also why we love her so very much.

LOVING FLY

It is sometimes difficult to find Fly sitting still. And it is even more difficult to find him with a lap that we may sleep on. But he sometimes sleeps, and we share his bed at night, and his scent fills us up. It is, perhaps, his constant absence that causes us to miss him so very much.

L O V I N G   M O M

We have mentioned how closely Mom resembles our own mother? This makes it very easy to love her. It does not make sense to try and explain it with logic. Love cannot always be explained in this way. Sometimes, love just is.

L O V I N G   S C R A T C H

Scratch? We have a feeling that whatever we might say about him will get changed in the end. He is a bit of a riddle. He is able to ignore us for great stretches of time, and we appreciate this quality about him, and it makes us want to be near him when he is alone, reading quietly on the bed. He is able to lie there on the bed and read and we can approach him and lie near him and he may reach out and scratch just the right place and then return to his reading without becoming obnoxious about the scratching.

We are able to sleep then, quite near him, without being bothered for some time.

He is also the Lap most likely to use the brush. He especially brushes us after we have just jumped up to eat, and this is somewhat annoying, but he means well. His meaning well and his stillness are two of the qualities that make him easy to love.

CHILDFRIEND

The Lap children have a friend who often visits. We do not mind him, but he attends to us too much (he is not *our* friend, you see—he is a friend of the Lap children). He picks us up and tries to hold us. He is too gentle, really, and his touch causes us anxiety, so we stretch out our body and move as if to free ourselves. He lets us have our way and says, "My cat doesn't do that. She lets me hold her all day if I want." We understand some of this. We understand that this means he thinks we are unusual. But we are not the one that is unusual. It is his relationship with his Othercat that is unusual. If he tries to force this relationship onto us, we will not reciprocate. We do not mind this Childfriend, as we said, but we will not allow ourselves to be made into something we are not.

THE MAIL CARRIER

As with many things, the dogs do not understand the mail carrier. The mail carrier visits the house nearly every day. He is a messenger, and he delivers odors and news from many parts of the neighborhood. To the dogs, this means he is a stranger and must be barked at and encouraged to leave. But when the mail carrier visits, we hope to be outside so as to receive his news. We follow him on his route throughout our neighborhood, and he sometimes reaches down to us as we sit just out of his reach. We understand he intends to pet us, but we do not want his scents and news to be diluted by our scent, so if he approaches, we move off.

Lately, though, the mail carrier has been leaving his Lap messages in the box, then dropping a handful of cat food on the steps. This tells us that he is one of the Most Intelligent Laps we have ever encountered. When we begin to eat the food, he scratches behind our ears, then moves off to finish his deliveries. He is not Scratch, but he is a Very Good Lap. We will try to be Out of Doors for his return every day.

PERSONAL SPACE

We reserve the right to invade what we understand the Laps call *personal space* at any moment, especially if they are currently sitting and thus forming an unused and perfectly suitable lap. Even better if they appear to be concentrating on some other object of the house, such as a newspaper or a book.

Furthermore, a Lap sitting and ignoring us altogether will be the first to receive our attention, because that Lap clearly understands cats and felinity. A direct stare and confrontation with a cat is a threat, but turning aside, as this visitor is currently positioned, is an invitation for intimacy.

"No," she says. "I don't like cats." So silly of her to say this, as we know she cannot mean it. There is no need to pretend. Her body tells us everything we need to know. "I'm allergic."

Whatever that means.

If a Lap should invade *our* personal space, however, we reserve the right to leave a claws-out, bright-red stripe (or three or four) on its face, its arm, its leg, or wherever we deem necessary in accordance with International Feline Law (which may be written according to our needs, whenever necessary).

PUPPY

What is this creature? It appears to be some form of dog, but somehow more full of curiosity, more full of pounce and roll and shuffle.

What will we do?

Leap!

FISHBOWL

Fish are a kind of prey, yet the Laps keep a fish in a bowl on a small table near the window. It is not important why

they do this. There is no good answer to a question like "Why do you keep a fish in a bowl in your house?" There is no answer to this question that could make any kind of sense.

In any case, we do not mind. We rather enjoy watching the fish. It is a different sort of motion from the motion of any other creature we have known.

Furthermore, when the Laps are not in the house we sometimes practice the fishswipe by putting our paws up on the rim of the bowl, reaching them into the water briefly, and pulling them out again quickly. We only practice the fishswipe once or twice at a time because, as you may have noticed, the fish lives in water. Water is no place for a cat. We practice the fishswipe because *we never know* when we might need to use it. If we were to be trapped outside for several weeks, for instance, and all there was to eat was a fish . . . We do not like to think of it, but the possibility exists. So we practice.

THE SQUIRREL

There is not just one squirrel. There are many. But there is also The Squirrel. The Squirrel We Chase. The Squirrel who lives on despite our having chased him across the street and into the yard, where he spends most of his time in the tree. Some squirrels can be caught, and we have caught them, and some squirrels we ignore, because we are tired, or because it is too much trouble to chase an especially fast squirrel. But this squirrel escapes far too often, and *we have had it* with this squirrel.

We have considered giving up, but we do not give up. We never give up. We watch for The Squirrel every day, and he appears to be most active in the morning, so we attempt to be Out of Doors every morning. About this time.

Just yesterday we saw The Squirrel. We watched him begin to cross the street, carrying a seed or other squirrel food in his mouth, and we had been watching and waiting for an opportunity like this. It is one of the things we do. We watch and wait for long periods, listening to the wind, picking up the sounds of small creatures and insects and the music of the earth.

The Squirrel was moving very near at hand, and we had but a moment to decide: to wait, to stalk, or to chase.

We chose, as may be evident from this story, the latter—to chase. We are, over short distances, faster than the squirrel, especially when he is burdened with squirrel food. We were able to overtake him in a moment, before he had even entirely crossed the street. We were not distracted by the curb or the grass or the sidewalk. We batted at him, just enough to swipe his tail aside, but he was not deterred, and he scampered onto the curb, across the sidewalk, and through the white picket fence without hesitation.

We now recognize our error. We could easily have jumped to the top of the fence and pounced from above, had we thought to do so before overtaking The Squirrel, before then overtaking the fence at full speed, before discovering that even at full speed we do not fit between the slats of the fence. It had not occurred to us to test the gaps between the pickets before now, so we had not tested them, and now we discovered that these openings really are too small, even for a creature giving chase, making themselves sleek and fast to catch a creature that had no trouble at all squeezing through.

We would have done so—jumped to the top of the fence—even then, leaping toward The Squirrel's domain, had we not now been so dizzy, so troubled by gravity.

The white picket fence is The Squirrel's secret

weapon, and he has apparently been saving it until this moment.

He is a clever squirrel, and we wonder, sometimes, if he is actually prey or if he has evolved from his squirrel companions into something other than squirrel.

No matter. We will make it seem as if running into this fence was exactly what we intended.

"What squirrel?" we might say if you asked. "We were just testing this fence." We will slink off in the opposite direction, wondering if the rabbit is Out of Doors at the neighbor's house.

RABBIT

There is a rabbit who lives in the house next door to the yard where The Squirrel lives. Yes, you heard us correctly. The rabbit lives Indoors. We did not know it was possible (or appropriate) for a rabbit to live Indoors, but this one does, and though we still do not think it appropriate to keep a rabbit this way, we are not in charge of what species Laps choose to make their companions.

The rabbit is not the same as the rabbits we have chased near our home. It is a different, fatter, unconcerned rabbit. When we approach the rabbit's yard, when we jump onto a post of the rabbit's fence (we do not believe it is possible for a rabbit to jump onto a fence, so we wonder why there is one to begin with—what is its purpose if there is no cat to patrol the perimeter?), the rabbit does not move. He appears to see us, but he is unconcerned. And though we generally believe rabbits to be of the prey type of animal, we do little more than watch this rabbit.

Why? In part because the rabbit appears to have no fear of us. There is no sport in attacking an animal that shows no fear. An animal that will not run from us. One that we will not have to chase.

Also, we wonder about this rabbit. Given that he shows no fear, does he know something that we don't? Does he have some special skill or weapon that we cannot appreciate from the top of the fence?

We have explored the rabbit's yard when he is Indoors, but we have not found any sort of weapon. Still, we are cautious. We only approach the rabbit in full view of him, and we do not make any sudden or threatening moves.

Someday we will discover what it is he knows, if anything. We spend a great deal of time Out of Doors just watching this rabbit. Perhaps a less-cautious Othercat will approach while we observe, and the rabbit will be forced to use his knowledge against the intruder, and we will be witness to his hidden source of empowerment. Until then, we will do as we always do. We will wait patiently, and watch.

MOUSE

Where is the mouse? There *was* a mouse. Have we seen the mouse today? Or was that yester- day? If a mouse comes to us, as the less intelligent of the mice sometimes do, espe- cially at night, when we are so still that it is almost as if we are not there, is it okay to give chase, or should we wait until the mouse is moving away? Can we attack when there is no sport in it?

We are not sure we can. So we won't. Not this time, anyway. Maybe next.

Go away, mouse. Go and hide.

BIRDS

Birds are considered prey. We have very few friends that are birds. In fact, we are having trouble thinking of any friends at all who are birds. We have heard of cats that tolerate chickens, but this is not exactly what we would call friendship. And anyway, we hardly think of chickens as birds.

We do not chase birds as prey because we are hungry, or because we need to eat birds, but we chase and catch them and prey on them because of the movement of their wings, because of their flapping and fluttering and flying about. Have you seen this? Can you prevent yourself from chasing them? From approaching with stealth and then batting them out of the air? Laps can apparently resist the birds. There must be something broken about their makeup that nullifies this attraction. (There is obviously more than one thing broken about the makeup of the Laps, but for the most part it is easy to ignore their brokenness so long as they continue to fill our food bowl when requested to do so.)

We do not always care to eat a bird once we have caught it. We bring it back to the house, to the Laps, to teach or to take their praise.

See what we did? Could you resist this bird?

Look at how lovely. What should we do with it now?

The Laps do not always know.

"What on earth?"

See?

"Not again. No. Stop. Give me that."

It seems they do not know exactly what to do with it either. We believe its wing, and perhaps its neck, has been broken. Once Scratch has freed the bird from us, we run into the house and go to our food bowl to wait for some reward.

It takes some time now before Scratch notices us. He is busy doing whatever it is he has to do with the bird. We don't know what it is he does with the bird, but it hardly matters. It is his now. Once it has stopped moving, it's hardly worth even thinking about.

Now then. Where is that reward?

7

EAT AND DRINK

You may think it unwise to rely so heavily on the companionship of Laps, especially when it comes to provisions. We do not find it so unwise. In general, Laps are trustworthy, if often forgetful and difficult to train, but they are also able to obtain food that is simply impossible for a cat to procure without assistance. For example: canned tuna fish. Have you ever seen a cat of any size catch a tuna fish? No, you have not. Chicken? Though it is possible for a cat to catch and kill a chicken, it is unwise, as the average chicken is a vicious beast that we prefer to avoid.

We can always find our own water, of course, but why bother? The Laps have mastered the use of the faucets. All of the faucets. Even those in the bathtubs. And from the faucets water flows freely and at will, much as it does from a waterfall.

The only trouble with our reliance on the Laps is when our will conflicts with theirs. But it is a minor trouble. The Laps are usually quick enough to do our bidding, recognizing and rearranging their priorities when necessary. And when they are not sufficiently compliant, we punish them by withholding our companionship. Though they are stubborn and often willful, with sufficient persistence, the Laps can and should be taught.

IN THE COMPANY OF LAPS

We wish that one of the Laps would hurry up and go into the bathroom (Scratch, maybe, because he spends the most time there) to relieve itself, because until they do, we cannot partake of the food placed in the dish on the shelf near the shower because there is no food there until it is placed there by one of the Laps (a task they will not remember to perform until we follow them into the bathroom to notify them of the absence of food).

We should hope that they understand our needs from past experience, but though they do have some feline qualities, they are not creatures of the highest intellect and therefore apparently do not often learn from experience. We will stand by the door to the bathroom and wait for them, and perhaps vocalize our complaint. When Scratch comes to us and we lead him into the bathroom and jump to the shelf where he fills the food bowl, he looks there and says, "I already fed you, you silly cat." We begin to eat, but once he has said, "I already fed you, you silly cat," he leaves the bathroom to return to whatever ill-conceived activity he was occupied with before entering the bathroom. We eat, now finally thankful that he came into the bathroom and there was food so we may eat and be fed, until we realize that he is no longer in the bathroom, and this concerns us because if he leaves the bathroom there will be nobody here to fill the food bowl.

Do we really have to do this again?

We eat for a few moments, then return to the living room. We rub our face against the sofa and *purr*, scent-marking and making a racket all the while. We sit near Scratch and once again vocalize our complaint. And again we vocalize our complaint. "What?" he says. "What do you want?" Again he proves himself incapable of understanding us.

We need you in the bathroom to fill the food bowl.

Scratch will return to the bathroom soon, and this time we follow him in instead of leading the way, and he will point to the food bowl and say, "Look, it's right there."

We know this already. So long as he is here, the food is here. Obviously. Does he not know his role in this?

We eat again for a few moments, but he has left us

alone again. A few more moments we eat. And that will be enough for now. We will wait. Until the next time someone enters the bathroom, we will sleep near the heat register.

In the Morning

You have not fed us yet. "Wreow!" *You have not fed us yet.* "Wreow!"

"Kitty, I put food in your bowl last night."

You have not fed us yet. "Wreow!"

"Look, come on. Did you even look in your bowl?"

Good. Food is coming. Food is coming. We will not starve to death. We will not die this morning for lack of food.

"Look. In here. Did you look in here?"

Put food in the bowl, please. There is no food in the bowl. "Wreow!"

"Jump up. Come on. Come look in the bowl."

No food yet. Why not fill the bowl? What is keeping you?

Leap! *What? Yes! Of course! The food is there.* That *food. Eating. Eating, yes.*

"You know what? You are the most ridiculous of cats."

They feed us this way sometimes. They bring us here and manage to put the food in the bowl without our seeing them do it. Without first getting the food out of the container and pouring it into the bowl. How they do it does not matter. What matters is that the food is here now, this moment. We will not die this morning. Nobody will die this morning.

Grateful? Yes. But sometimes we wonder why the Laps don't just put food in the bowl before we go to bed so it would be here in the morning whenever we wanted it.

Perhaps the Laps like to feel needed. This is their way of showing it.

CAT WATER

There is a bowl of water set out near our food that we assume is meant for us to drink. However, we do not drink from this water except when extremely thirsty. This water smells foul, of the chemicals used to clean the dish, perhaps. Or maybe there are chemicals in the water itself. We test this water once in a while and yes, it smells and even tastes of undrinkable chemicals that we recognize as the same odors that come from the dishwasher when it has been recently run. Does Mom not smell the detergent in the water? Are they not able to properly wash these dishes so that they are no longer coated in detergent?

Perhaps this water is not really meant for us. Perhaps

this water is meant to keep the dog away from our food by tricking the dog into thinking there is detergent here instead of food and water. If this is their intention, it isn't working, because there is the dog, trying to decide if she can quite reach the bowl of food if she stands on her hind legs.

EATING GRASS

Yes, we eat grass. We would rather not eat grass, but when our stomach feels as it does today, we eat grass. This does not immediately make our stomach feel better, but it does make us feel as if something is moving inside us, as if whatever it is that is causing this discomfort will eventually pass. So we eat the grass and wait for the discomfort to pass. We kindly ask you—and you know who you are—to stop cutting the grass. It is much more difficult to eat one blade at a time when it is cut so short.

EATING HOUSEPLANTS

When we are Indoors, we sometimes settle for the houseplants. Many of the houseplants serve the same purpose as the grass in front of the house. Too often, when we eat of the houseplants, we hear something quick and loud from above that sounds a bit like "Thou shalt not eat of the houseplants!" If we are not quick to move away from the houseplants at this time, we will receive a burst of water on our backs. Having been caught eating the houseplants also might cause the Laps to put us outside, where we can eat the grass instead. It is therefore a good idea to eat the houseplants, whether we are prepared for the consequences or not.

It is better than this feeling in our stomach, anyway—the feeling that we will not be able to eat anymore, ever. The grass always helps this feeling go away, by either moving through us or back out of us.

Laps call this moving back out of us *vomit*. Or sometimes *hairball*. We don't care what they call it, especially if they are the ones who will be cleaning it up. It is very difficult to cover the vomit by digging in the carpet. The carpet does not cover the vomit well. We feel better now that it's out of us, and that's all that matters.

CAT FOOD BOWL

We are always surprised that when we eat food from this bowl, it does not taste at all like fish. This fish printed on the side of the bowl? It must be a very tricky fish. At first we thought it was a label for what the bowl contained, but this cannot be true. When we are finished eating, we look again, and it is still there. It will still be there the next time we eat. And still the food will taste nothing like fish.

What is the purpose of this fish? Is it a representation of what we are not eating? Is it a mistake made by the manufacturer of the bowl?

We are not bothered too much. While we eat, we . . . um . . . what were we saying?

MOUSE AS FOOD

We could treat the mouse as food, if we wished to do so. We have the ability and the resources. And the teeth. But very often we do not have the desire. The mouse might be good enough to eat. The mouse could even be delicious. But we choose the food in the dish on the shelf near the shower. This food is not as fun as the mouse. But it is easier. And generally more tasty. And allows Laps the illusion of our dependence upon them.

We have tried to use the mouse as a teaching tool, but this has been even more unsuccessful than teaching the Laps with the bird. When we bring the mouse onto the porch, there is an even more violent and distressed reaction than when we bring birds. We still do it, at times, but our Laps have learned almost nothing from it.

E G G

We have been known, upon occasion, to eat a raw egg, cracked into a bowl for us in the early morning before most of the Laps are awake. We do not eat all of the egg, but we eat enough to know that if we are ever in a chicken coop, we will not be chasing after chickens, but we *will* be looking for eggs.

Yes, they are that good. And easier, of course, to hunt down.

T U N A

Are you kidding us? Tuna? We rarely rarely—if ever—get more than a tiny chunk of tuna. The first few weeks we were here we got tuna three or four times. They were being nice to us, we think. Spoiling us. Hoping to imprint on us the fact that they are family.

This may have, in fact, worked quite marvelously. We were indeed imprinted as such, but we are not sure it was the tuna that did it. Still, when we hear the can opener opening a can (and we can tell the difference in tonality between a can of tuna and a can of green beans), we are immediately at the feet of whoever it is that is opening the can. Once in a while we will snatch a dropping or two of the tuna. But *so* rarely. And anyway, we're not sure if we actually like the tuna anymore.

Oh, that's not true. We love it. Keep opening the cans.

But know that as much as we love the tuna, we also come running because we know we are supposed to come running. It pleases everyone when we come running.

Even us.

Waiting in the Kitchen for a Dropped Morsel

Whenever you are ready to drop that (we believe we heard the sound of a tuna can opening, yes?), we are ready to pounce, to accept it as an offering, to forgive whatever it was we were going to forgive.

We lick our chops.

Here it comes.

It is coming now.

Now?

Please?

Will you drop it already?

Dog Water

If there are no dogs near the dog water bowl, we may drink from the dog water bowl. There are no unpleasant odors associated with the dog water bowl. Though while we drink from the dog water bowl we are always filled with some minor anxiety. We are always thinking to ourselves, "There's a dog right behind us, isn't there?" Even when we do not otherwise sense a dog behind us, we are thinking this. When we sense movement behind us, we turn quickly and disappear.

B E D S I D E   W A T E R

Every night there is a new glass of water on the table beside the bed where Mom looks at books and also sleeps. This water never smells of strange odors or chemicals (it must somehow get cleaner in the dishwasher or is in some way made of a better material that does not hold the scent of the detergent) and Mom sometimes drinks from this water, so it must be for drinking (and she leaves her scent on the glass, of course, which makes it that much more attractive). We drink from this water while she is looking at books or while she is sleeping. If she is looking at books she makes a noise. "Shoo," she says. "That's my water."

It is difficult to drink from this water if Mom drinks any of the water before we find it first. If she drinks first, the water is far away from the rim of the glass, and it is therefore difficult to drink, though not impossible, because as a last resort we can tip the glass over so that the water spills onto the floor and we drink as it moves away into the carpet. This is a last resort, because this also tends to wake the Laps, who are not glad to hear the noise or to clean the water from the floor.

It has been a long time since we have resorted to tipping this glass over. She has been very good at keeping it full lately. Which confirms for us that she is capable of being taught at long last. And thank goodness. All our work has been useful.

8

REST AND SLEEP

Rest and sleep are two of the most important aspects of our lives. We have gone entire days without eating, but we doubt we could go an entire day without sleeping. In fact, if memory serves us, the reason we have gone entire days without eating is that we were otherwise engaged in sleep.

When we sleep, it is not so much a matter of our needing to sleep per se as it is a need to shut down all sensory input. We do not need to feel tired to sleep. But when we've been receiving data all day, we need to turn off the world as much as possible. We turn down the volume, if you

will. When we sleep, the sensory input stops as much as it ever will for a cat. It must be quieted, or we would likely go insane.

If you have ever met one, you know there is nothing more dangerous than an insane cat. For such a cat we recommend a dark room, a favorite jacket thrown on a bed, and twenty solid hours of sleep. It turns out some forms of insanity can be cured.

DAY

It is daytime. This is the perfect time of day to sleep. During the day. When it is bright and there is sun shining. Sun shining provides warmth. Sun shining may provide warmth either inside the house or outside the house. And warmth provides sleep. It activates sleep. It causes sleep, sometimes. It makes the clock in us shut down and we sleep. An entire day can pass, light all the day through and sun shining on us, and we will sleep through it.

LASER PRINTER

The laser printer is a Lap contraption, and it serves some purpose for them, especially Scratch. It makes paper, we think. Or eats it. Or, perhaps, finds it intolerable, and so spits it out, at which point Scratch removes and admires it. But this is not important. Because the laser printer serves a Higher Purpose, for when it is finished making or eating or spitting paper, it is usually quite warm and is therefore a fine place to lie (though not to sleep, because it is never long before we are interrupted by the spitting paper), especially when we have just been lifted and dropped from a lap. When we have just been dropped from a lap that happens to be near the laser printer, the chances of the laser printer's being warm are high, because Scratch has likely just woken the laser printer, which causes it to warm up. Furthermore, the scent of the laser printer after it has just been used (a scent that makes us think that the laser printer might be used for recycling rather than making or eating the paper) means only one thing: *warm rest lie (possible sleep but shouldn't sleep)*. Sometimes we go to the laser printer room because we are following this scent. We are drawn there in the same way we are drawn to anything necessary.

When we are in the laser printer room, we are sometimes distracted, however, by the presence of the computer monitor, our preference for which obviously overrides any preference we might have had for the laser printer.

COMPUTER MONITOR

When we remember the computer monitor (upon entering the laser printer room), we are overtaken with sleepiness, and we jump to the desk and *purr* and walk across the keyboard (whether it is being used or not) and rub against the computer monitor to leave our scent there (no sense having some other creature believe the computer monitor is theirs to use at will) and turn and walk across the keyboard and leave our scent on the opposite corner of the computer monitor.

"Okay, Kitty," says Scratch. He lifts us and sets us on the floor, at which time we jump back up and approach the computer monitor, savoring what we are about to do.

Up. Up on top of the monitor. So. Very. Warm. And

full of the scent of sleep. The knowledge of sleep. The approach of sleep. The sound of sleep invading us. The taste of sleep. It is so lovely. This sleep. Full of dreams of scooping fish from a pond. Many fish scooped out onto the shore of the pond. Fish on which to gorge ourselves. So gorged we are soon sleepy. Sleepy even in our dreams, ready for sleep even in our dreams, another dream embedded inside the dream of fishing. A dream of . . . what?

Our dream ends in one of the following ways.

1. Scratch wakes us and lifts us again, setting us either on the desk or the floor and saying, "Okay, Kitty. I need that." Then he retrieves something from the top of the computer monitor, something we were apparently sleeping on. Could he have not retrieved it before we climbed up there and fell asleep?

2. We wake and find the light turned dim, the room vacant, and fish swimming on the computer monitor. We attempt to dip our paw into the black waters of the monitor's pond, but the fish are behind glass and there is no apparent opening. The computer monitor doubles as this fishbowl when nobody is using it.

   Where do these fish hide when Scratch *is* using the computer?

3. Fall and jolt. A serious and severe jolt. And we are no longer on the computer monitor but scrabbling for purchase on the desk, trying to determine where exactly the world has gone and how to return to reality, and then again just as suddenly jumping before we know who or where we are to some flat surface, to sit and stare and regain our composure, to lick and groom our paws (they will certainly smell of fish) and wonder what it is that Scratch is laughing at. We look at him with lazy eyes, then walk slowly from the room as if we have someone to meet in another part of the house. Someone we have scheduled for just this time of day, whatever time of day it is. It is surely teatime, is it not? We are taking tea with Mom and Kittengirl. Where are they? A dish of milk would be perfect just now. Are they coming? Did they forget about teatime?

In the Sun

When we lie down to sleep and the light is slanting through the room onto us (so warm—the Laps call it Sun-Light), we dream of the Home Place, the Running and Dancing Place where Prey is as Big as Us or Even Bigger. But when we wake, the light has moved or even disappeared.

Who moves it? Do the Laps move it? Do they need it somewhere else? And how do they do this? We would like to be able to take it back when we want. That would be a Useful Skill for Cats, to have complete control over the sun.

If we could figure out the physics of this movement, we would bring the light onto ourselves whenever we napped. But we've never actually seen anyone move the light. It only seems to move as we sleep.

Laps can be very clever, and we haven't caught them stealing the light from us, though we suspect it is them because they also have control of other lights both Indoors and Out of Doors—light from the lampshades and the ceilings (this is not the same sort of light as the Sun-Light, alas, or we would learn to use the lampshade and ceiling lights ourselves).

We respect them for their cleverness, but we are annoyed nonetheless.

T W O   O F   T H E   B E S T   P L A C E S   T O   S L E E P

There are Sunny Spots, and there are stairs. Sunny Spots are preferable because we will always be warm in a Sunny Spot and we will dream the dreams of the Place That Is Home, though we have not been there—it is like a memory of a home, though stronger, more vivid, more desirable.

Stairs are also lovely because we will receive notice when a Lap moves up or down the stairs as if to fill our food bowl (or as if to escape where they have been set at a task), and we may proceed to said food bowl in haste. In rare instances, there may be a Sunny Spot upon the stairs, in which case we will take up residence there until the Sunny Spot has moved away (as it always does) and we wake to the sound of movement on the stairs, of a human prepared to feed us, or a human who is not prepared but must be prodded to feed us. We will prod them, and we will be fed.

Oh. And there are portions of beds that have at some time been slept on by a Lap. The beds smell of the Laps, and the odor is not unpleasant. It reassures and settles us. It makes us believe we will never again be left outside during a thunderstorm.

Were we left outside during a thunderstorm, or did we just hear of a cat to whom this happened?

We are unsure. But the beds reassure us nonetheless.

PILLOW

This soft and malleable place is full of the odor of sleep, more than all other places on the bed, and it thus deserves

its own discussion. We knead our paws into the pillow and rub our face against it, and we are reminded of sleep and family, and when we lie down and curl our tails up against ourselves, we are halfway there, to the odor of our own sleep, and sometimes if we sleep here we will share the dreams of the last Lap to use the pillow, and that is a truly fine experience, to know what it is to be so tall in the world, to wander through life with our head above everything else. And, especially, to be able to approach the doors with so much confidence, to reach out and turn the knob, to open, ourselves, just turn the knob and open the door.

THE SENSE OF SLEEP

There are places to sleep in any given space that we know have never been slept in or on, because we do not smell the odor of someone having slept there. But we also sense the sleep, the comfort and peace therein, and we find the position, the way in which to make the place work as a Place for Sleep.

We are geniuses of the bed, our bodies turned or

twisted or contorted or curled so as to snooze, drifting toward that Inner Land of Sleep.

MEDITATION

There are times when our eyes are closed, and we are in a sleeping position, when it may be assumed by others of our household that we are sleeping. Sometimes it may be true—we are sleeping. But sometimes we are not sleeping. And we are not resting. We are closing our eyes and turning inward. At the same time, turning outward. Some of us may perform the *purr* as we turn inward. The *purr* is a meditation technique, and we may invoke it at any time. Turning outward. Our breathing slows, and the rhythm of our breathing turns inward. Turning outward. Our eyes close against the outward light. Turning inward light. The sound of the light is us. Our inside becoming light. Is the world. Is the light of the universe. *Purr.*

If you wish, during this time, you may join us. At this time, we have joined you.

So join us. Come near and close your eyes and

purr, as we do. Turn inward, and outward. We entreat you.

L A P

Some laps are good for sleeping, or at least for resting, and we approach Laps with just such laps before all others. We know these laps instinctively, for there is a certain stillness to them, a way of spreading flat and soft and warm and waiting for us. We sense the sleep there, as if it is waiting for us to discover. We turn circles on such a lap and *purr* and knead the lap as if we might milk more comfort from it. And we lie. And if we have chosen the correct time on the correct lap (which we almost certainly have), we may sleep for many days before the lap moves, only rising (of course) to feed us. The value of such a lap is, as is well known, immeasurable.

S H A R E D   S L E E P

We always sleep more soundly under the spell and scent of another creature's breath, especially if that creature shares our sleep and our breath, thus sharing dreams, thus living in a world unimaginable while awake.

If we sleep with our head near the nose of the dog, for

instance, we may dream ourselves tall enough—and we drink from the toilet without the risk of slipping, of getting our paws wet and out of control, of continuing downward in a violent vortex of vanishing water. We simply approach the toilet and put our head in and drink.

If we sleep with our head near the foot of a Lap bed, we may dream of giving birth to a kitten—a litter of just one kitten—of licking the kitten from tip-top wisp of hair to ticklish toe, of listening to our kitten, a girl, *purr* as she suckles, as she giggles and gurgles, as she sleeps and wakes us. A foot in our belly. What?

If we sleep within the curl of an agreeable cat from our family, we may dream of walking in one direction and traveling in another. We may dream of flight, of not being able to come down from the air, floating but unable to do anything about it. Though this confuses both of us, we have shared the same dream, and when we wake, for a moment, we look at each other as if seeing and knowing the other for the first time, until one of us will recall that this is *our* bed, that this is *our* sleep, and we will hiss and jump and turn and claw a tail, run and turn and sit and wait, and wait, now tired again, yawning, waiting. For what, we don't quite know.

Perhaps we will sleep again, and there is a good chance the cat with whom we shared this dream will come to join us.

ON THE LAP BED
WITH OUR LAPS

On a bed. Asleep. The Laps gone utterly horizontal, as if their entire bodies were laps (though they tend to move too much in their sleep, so they are not as well suited for sleeping on when positioned and sleeping thus).

When we can hear the blood pulsing through another body, and the heat from that body is just warm enough to keep us thinking of our mother, that is when we sleep our deepest, but that is also when we are most likely to be awoken by the twitch of a foot, by a trip to the bathroom.

We will sleep with them for a little while so that we can experience this sort of sleep, but it never fails. We are too often interrupted. So we will return to the big puffy chair downstairs. The one that smells of all the beings of the house, all of them having sat or slept here at one time or another. It is like a Lap bed, where a Lap presents us with a lap, and though it is not as exquisite as the bed itself, it will do very well until morning.

WITH DOG

It is too difficult to sleep with Daydog. She cannot lie still and often rolls onto her back. So we will mostly discuss sleeping with Nightdog.

We allow Nightdog to sleep here with us (on the floorbed that she seems convinced is hers and hers alone) because she is warm. If Nightdog ceases to be warm, we will have her removed by Royal Decree (we will hiss and bat at her ears until she moves off the floorbed). If Nightdog cannot be still, she will be removed by Royal Biting of Ears. If Nightdog leaves us without first requesting dismissal, we will send a message for her to return. She will be punished by being required to lie still and be warm. Stop fidgeting. We are trying to sleep.

9

WORK AND PLAY

Play is a form of work, and we take work and play as seriously as any creature. We take play most seriously of all, as it is the most important form of work. Play makes us healthy and keeps us from becoming sick. Furthermore, play and how we play and with whom we play is what makes us who we are.

Therefore, if you notice that the ball of yarn has been strewn across the floor, please put the yarn back into the form of a ball and do not bother yourself with sighs and complaints. When we come back from the bathroom we do not want to see it in this mess. When it is in this mess it is danger-ous to cats because the ball of yarn is no longer useful as an

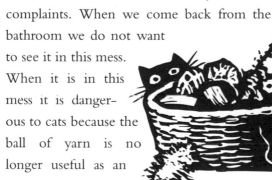

object of play, and there must be objects of play in every household. Dangerous to cats dilutes the importance of play precisely because the importance of play is diluted. A home in which the importance of play is diluted quickly deteriorates into a playless house, and this is a dangerous situation indeed.

Therefore we would not only ask that this yarn be returned to a ball without delay but that you fix the toilet roll in the bathroom. We've pulled all the paper out of it that we care to, and we won't be returning to the bathroom until it is ready for us once again.

Thank you.

LOOKING UP

We are watching for it. Is it always there or does it move? Where is it? We think we saw whatever it was up there, on that shelf, the one we have not yet discovered how to leap upon. We saw it there last time we saw it, whatever it was (and we need it, so we are watching for it). Right up there. Though it doesn't appear to be there now, does it? Where could it have gone? Does it move? Is it a living thing? Is it a static thing? How long before it returns?

What is it? Do you remember?

Also, as long we are looking up and have left ourself so

exposed, would you be so kind as to scratch under our chin?

S T A N D

Though we can stand up on our hind legs—to retrieve something high up, for instance, or to have a look at something out of our sight, or to make ourselves appear more powerful to an opponent—we do not like to do it for long, for we are too easily unbalanced, too easily toppled. We do not feel correct when standing this way. We feel as if we may flip over at any moment.

So we return to a crouch. To a curl. To a pounce. The world back the way it should be.

We will count on the Laps to be the tallest of the creatures in the household. Being low to the ground does have its benefits. Such as sleeping in small spaces.

That is what we will do now. Let us know if you see a Creature of Importance approaching outside of the window. We do like reports of these things. We just can't always be awake to be witness to them.

TOY ON A STRING

This thing again. How many times do we have to catch this thing? How many times before it stops moving forever? What on earth makes it so persistent? Is Scratch controlling it? If so, how? Is he at the other end of this tether somehow, making it move like a bird or other flying creature? How does he make it so birdlike if neither he nor the toy is a bird?

And why, even though the way it moves looks so very tasty, does its taste remind us instead of eating bark?

LAZY

Lazy? Did you say *lazy?* Were you referring to *us?*

Is this a joke?

We are not lazy. Quite the opposite. We perform some of the most important duties of the kingdom. We are figureheads, to be sure. But also diplomats. And protectors. Advisers. Greeters. Soldiers. Decision makers. And we do all this with relative stealth, so you call us lazy?

Unfair, we say. Indeed, we call you busybodies. It has been a long day today. Can you not leave us alone while we get some much-needed rest?

Many decisions to make. Many lives in our care. Much to do. To yawn. To protect.

F I G U R E H E A D

It may be thought that we have little or no control of the royal household, of the politics and occurrences within, that we are nothing but a beautiful showpiece. An ornament. A thing of beauty to be trotted out for weddings and funerals. But ask yourself this: Who makes the rules in your house that you must absolutely follow?

Such as: *Let us out.*

And also: *Let us in.*

Figurehead indeed.

D I P L O M A T S

We have been known, upon occasion, to be first in line when trouble comes knocking. We are an emergency notification creature. We will be sitting on a fencepost, for instance, when a strange Tomcat comes by (though we were expecting it, as Toms are incapable of minding their own business). We may take it upon ourselves to inform this Tomcat of his unwelcome status. It is easier to inform him than have him attempt to enter the yard—or, worse, the garage (or, even worse still, the house, though we are relatively certain that the Tom cannot operate the front door any better than we can).

That we have few unwanted entrances to the yard and garage and house, and even fewer violent confrontations regarding said entrances, is an indication of our skill at diplomacy.

SOLDIERS

Should the Tomcat insist, we may have to take up arms against him, and by opposing, send him on his way. Why? To sleep, of course. So the entire house may sleep. So as not to disturb their dreams.

We are soldiers. There will be no great intrusion while we are on watch. None whatsoever.

EDUCATORS

The greatest lesson we have ever tried to teach the Laps of the household is how to hunt. We know that they know how to obtain their own food by other methods, and we know that we will likely never go hungry as long as they continue to fetch and prepare food for us (it is their duty, after all), but as good proprietors of the household, we feel it is our duty to prepare them for the worst. Should the time come, they may have to hunt and kill their own food.

So we do as we would do with our kittens.

We go out. We find good prey. A mouse or a bird. We do not kill it. Not yet. First it must be a good lesson.

We bring it back to the house. Very often when we bring it back, the Laps sense that we have come with live prey. They apparently have good senses even though they rarely use them.

If it is Mom who comes to us, she calls out for Scratch, who apparently needs more lessons than the rest of the family.

"Can you come and see what your cat brought us?"

Scratch comes. He looks down at us with a confused expression. He apparently does not know what to do with the bird. This is why we have brought it for him. To teach him.

"Oh, God," he says. "Not another bird." And he swoops down as if to take the bird from us. As I said, he has good senses. Good instincts. He takes the bird from us. But then? Then we watch as he utterly botches it. He does not properly chase or pounce or take the bird in his mouth. He does not shake it or bat it or kill it. Once we saw him remove a bird to another part of the garden and set it free.

He set it free!

Perhaps we cannot teach the Laps how to hunt and kill. We hope the day will never come that they need to hunt for their own food, for they will surely perish.

ADVISERS

We never hesitate to let our opinion on any matter be known. It is sometimes difficult to get our precise meaning across, but for the most part we have little trouble communicating with whomever we want.

For instance, right now we are in favor of reducing the number of dogs in the household. The household appears to be overrun with dogs, and we are spending a great deal of time Out of Doors so as not to be molested quite so vociferously. When Indoors, however, we make our opinion known to the Laps, who seem to have some small amount of control over the dogs.

"Don't worry," they say. "They're not all staying. We're just watching them for a friend."

We sometimes wonder why the Laps don't come to us earlier for advice. We could have told them this was not a good idea, that the infant dogs would urinate and otherwise sully the household.

Dogs do not always—in fact, practically never—offer us the respect we deserve. It is not that they are incapable of offering such respect. It is simply that they tend to defer to the Laps. Luckily, Scratch is aware of this and will often convey our advice to the dogs. As we have said, they sometimes listen to him. And thank goodness. They would otherwise be uncontrollable and intolerable. As it is, they are merely a great nuisance. Just because we are an excellent adviser does not mean anybody will listen to us. Some things have to be learned by experience.

GREETERS

Style 1

We never fail to greet whoever might come to the door and knock or ring or simply enter. When we greet, we scentmark the door and may scentmark the newcomer's legs as well (depending upon our familiarity with the entering party). But we will at the very least greet whoever has come to call. Every call deserves some form of greeting, and we are especially good at this chore, as we are obviously the most beautiful and hospitable creature of the household. We never fail to receive the compliments of our post, and it is a matter of great pride for us, pride being one of the Great Virtues of Being Feline.

Style 2

We would like to point out that while some of us greet in Style 1, others are more cautious. Before greeting the new visitor, we might actually hide under a chair. Eventually we will greet the visitor. It might take us a few weeks to warm up, but we will make our way out and work our way up to it and eventually crouch beneath the chair the visitor is sitting in. About to greet the visitor. Any moment.

Are you sure the visitor is not dangerous?

DECISION MAKERS

There is no hemming and hawing when it comes to our making a decision. The longest it ever takes us to decide yes or no is a few moments, and you can see it happening. For instance, we may be sitting upon the table outside the front window, where the Laps sometimes eat their meals on warm summer evenings, and be spotted by Fly, who goes to the door and opens it for us to come inside. It had not occurred to us, really, until that moment, that our sitting upon the table might be interpreted as a request to open the door. But here it is, time to decide. Do we want to go inside?

We lean forward on our front paws, still undecided, then leap forward, and step slowly through the door, scentmarking the passageway with our jowls as we pass.

In a few moments, after having passed from the front room of the house into the kitchen, then into the bathroom and now back to the front, we must decide again, and we sit for half a moment this time, then go to the door and stand near it, vocalizing our *mrrreow.* We wish to return to the Out of Doors, to sit upon the table that is now receiving some small amount of sun. To lie there, perhaps, and sleep.

Fly does not appear to notice us. He flies up the stairway.

Fine. We will find some other Lap to let us out. Perhaps Scratch. He is using the computer and laser printer, is he not? Good. It is easy to get his attention when he is thus positioned. We simply walk across the keyboard, and he is forced to notice us. To do something with us. To let us back outside. We have made our decision, and we want to go outside now.

Once a decision is made, it sometimes takes a great deal of effort to have that decision acted upon.

EXPLORATION

There are places in the house that change, somehow, from explored places to unexplored places. When an explored place becomes an unexplored place, then it must be explored. Once it has been explored properly, and once we have moved away from the explored place (for it is now an explored place because we have explored it), we notice that because we have left the room or gone outside, it may again be an unexplored place and, again, we will have to explore it. We may look inside and say, "This was here before? Are you *sure* it was like this before we went outside?" Indeed. The entire room has become unexplored. We will, of course, explore it.

PLAY WITH DOG

What would this house be without Daydog? It would be very quiet. It would be a better place for sleep. It would be a better place to meditate, to rest and listen to the *purr* of the universe.

But at the same time, it would not speak so much of the complete universe.

We are not exactly sure what it is inside us that makes us want to do what it is we do with Daydog, but this is what we do with Daydog.

When Daydog is quite still (perhaps asleep), we will approach her, and we will roll onto our back, and Daydog will understand that this means we are ready to play. She will jump up and put her mouth around our head and make a noise like a dog will do, a kind of whining and growling noise like only a dog can make, and though it is a hideous and earth-shattering noise, this noise and this action somehow speak to us, almost as if there is some connection between dog and cat, as if there might be some kinship. And though many cats (and many dogs) will deny this kinship, and though some have seen this action between dog and cat as dangerous or even immoral, we believe that this kinship exists, and we encourage it.

Mostly.

Except when it annoys us.

Stupid dog.

P L A Y   W I T H   D A Y D O G ' S   T A I L

Sometimes we are so filled with joy in Daydog's presence (especially if she is lying on the floor and her tail is moving to and fro) that we will pounce on her moving tail (to and fro). For there is no movement more attractive to a pounceable cat as the movement of a dog's tail (especially one with lots of feathering, as feathering is very birdlike and attractive and oh so irresistible). It is as attractive as a rabbit's hop, at least.

So far as we can tell, there are only two disadvantages to pouncing on the dog's tail.

The first disadvantage is that there is a dog attached to the dog's tail, and as much as we love to play with the dog and have her put her mouth over our head and make the awful noise, we are rarely in the mood to have her put her mouth over our head and make the awful noise when we are in the mood to pounce on her tail. In this case, after we have pounced on her tail we will have to seek shelter.

The second disadvantage to pouncing on the dog's tail is that we cannot eat it or even carry it away with us. This may seem obvious to some, but, pouncing as we are on the tail of a dog, we sometimes do not think, at first, that the object we are pouncing on will not be edible or movable once we have pounced on it. Only once we have pounced and the dog has turned to see what has pounced does it occur to us that we will not be able to eat or carry away what we have just pounced on, and we will likely not be able to spend more time pouncing on the tail either, for the dog has discovered us and will turn and find us there and will return a pounce (which we are not, as we said, in the mood for at this moment).

This is a good time for us to jump up onto the piano.

ALERT

Did you hear that? Was it a gazelle? We are finely tuned to the hoofbeat of the gazelle, you know. We have yet to see or smell or actually know what a gazelle looks like, but the hoofbeat, yes. Was that the hoofbeat?

Or no. A car door slamming shut. Again. Drat.

The car door fools us often. Have you heard a car door slamming shut? It sounds almost exactly like a gazelle. We are almost sure of it.

10

CHI

Chi is the energy that flows through a cat (or any creature, for that matter). It is the energy of the universe. If you have ever seen a cat lying in the grass, waiting almost without breathing, watching and listening as the bird in the bush hops from branch to branch, then darting forward, almost without effort, into the bush with a single swipe, and then returning to ground with the bird, you may begin to understand the power of chi. It makes us capable of great things.

It moves us.

But it also keeps us quite still.

THE WORLD

The way we imagine the world is the way the world is. Furthermore, the world does not exist until we imagine it. It is good that we are here. It is good for the Lap children and all animals that we are here, for without us the

world would not exist as it is. It would be very different, being imagined only by Lap children and other creatures (such as dogs, who do not have the sort of imagination it takes to imagine the world in a proper fashion—surely if there were only dogs to imagine the world, the entire world would be edible).

Without us, for instance, we are certain there would be no laser printer or computer monitor.

In return? We ask only for a spot on the sofa where the sun slants through during the day (or on the computer monitor, of course, a place full of warmth and light and sometimes fish). This is our sun. Our computer monitor. Our unoccupied lap to be filled up with us, to be fulfilled by a human hand scratching just behind our ears.

Yours and ours. We imagine. We dream. The world becomes.

CAT PHYSICS

It may appear to you that we are resting, but without notice we may disappear from wherever it is we have been prone and reappear on top of the refrigerator as if transported there by a quantum, subatomic feline accelerator. When seeking out the mysteries of the universe, we advise you to ask us for our assistance.

We may refuse our assistance, but you will do yourself no favor by neglecting to ask.

MEOW

What does the sound that we make *mean?*

How do you respond to the sound of the rain on the rooftops? The wind in the grass? The river's kiss? How do you hold the scent of a flower? Do you hold it best with your hands, your eyes, or the fur standing up on your neck?

It obviously means whatever the situation requires. At the door, it means *In* or *Out,* or, at the very least, *Open.* Near the food dish, it means *Fill.* In your lap, it most certainly means *Scratch behind ears.* It may also mean *Now. Right now. You are taking too long.*

LAWS

We are not opposed to breaking the laws of sleep and physics. Laws are, after all, meant to be broken.

What are the laws of sleep and physics?

They are unknown. They are mystery. We do not understand them because we are not meant to understand them.

This does not mean that they do not exist. It simply means that we do not and will not ever know when we are breaking these laws. Neither will we know when we are obeying them.

Better not to ask whether we are breaking or obeying. Better to find a high place to sleep outside the view of the Laps so as not to be disturbed. To bend the light around us until it is time to wake up. To become invisible. To float three inches above the bed as we sleep.

PURR HARMONY

The *purr* is the sound of meditation. It is the sound of the universe. The universe may be said to *purr*, and when we *purr* we are in harmonious synchrony with the universe. At times we attempt to draw the Laps into our synchrony. It seems to calm them. It seems to change them momentarily. And although they are not apparently capable of complete harmony with the universe—as we are—they can at least feel this glimmer of it. This momentary music. This *purr*.

A WARE

Our awareness of the members of our household—the Laps and Dogs—is exhausting. It is a bit like our awareness of Our Kittens. It is a bit like our awareness of All Creatures in the Sphere of Our Consciousness. All the creatures. The dogs. The piano. Even the Creatures That Seldom Move, such as the piano. The farther away these beings are in physical proximity, the more exhausting our experience of them. For we continue to experience them, to track and watch out for them. When this exhausts us, we may sleep in a way that shuts out this continued experience, so as not to be woken, so as not to feel the movements of our world so closely.

Or we may request a kind of prolonged permanence of Those Who Move About—a Lap in a chair we would like to stay put. We ask that they *not move*. We lie upon the lap and in this way communicate our need for them to *not move*, our claws ready to enforce this permanence. Do not move. Not. Move. A muscle.

WANT

Do they not hear us? We are telling them. And telling them and telling them and telling them. We say it again and again, but they do not respond in a satisfactory manner. They are all about themselves sometimes, and we do all we can to get their attention, to get them to move. Hello? Do you not hear?

What is it we want?

Okay. We don't remember. But is that really important? Do you really need us to be so precise?

When you give it to us, we will know. And we will tell you then.

PRIDE

We have heard pride described as a thing not to be valued. But as a cat, we value pride, though we may define pride differently than most other creatures.

Pride is the thing that keeps us alive when we are in danger. Pride allows us to stay healthy when threatened. Pride keeps us from allowing our family, our home, to become endangered. We protect the household and teach our family and take care of all creatures that need care because, in part, of pride. We are proud of our family, of our home. We are proud of ourself. Of Fly and Kittengirl. We are proud that they know who they are, that they are able to see that flying and catlifting are part of who they are meant to be, of who they will always be, and they stay centered in that.

For us, pride is a virtue. Perhaps one that is often misunderstood, but nevertheless a virtue, and we carry it with us everywhere.

ART OF THE STRETCH

Cats are, as you may know, artistic beings, though not in the sense that Laps are artistic beings. We may paint or draw or sculpt, but only by accident. One of our greatest modes of expression is the stretch. If you have seen us in the grass, on our back, paws tossed outward thus, as far as our body will allow, then you already understand the beauty of this form. When you see a cat thus, do stop to appreciate the subtlety of expression, the slightest turn of paw, the gracefulness of position. Note our angle to the sun.

We have become this thing of beauty. Is that not an art?

This is what we sometimes call the readyroll position, which is not only beautiful but also useful when we need to roll away from imminent danger. It is also extremely good for the circulation.

ART OF IGNORE

Ignoring another cat in the same room as us is not just an art, it is a finely crafted skill, for we have to do it completely and absolutely. We must utterly ignore, and make as if there is no other cat in the room, has never been another cat in the room, will never be another cat in the room, and we have to perform this feat with utter concentration on where the other cat is located at all times, just in case of a pounce.

Utter concentration on, and complete ignorance of. It takes a great deal of practice. Every day we practice, if possible. If we live with another cat in the house? We practice for hours at a time.

INVISIBILITY

When necessary, when we absolutely need to be unseen and untouched, it is possible to make ourselves invisible. We do this, at times, when Scratch is calling for us at the front door.

"Here, Kitty Kitty Kitty."

We simply cannot be disturbed right now. We have things to meditate on. We have a world to consider. Lives that are our responsibility. We have to let some of the mechanisms of our day be at peace.

"Here, Kitty Kitty Kitty."

If he continues to call long enough, we will release our invisibility. He will reenter the house and close the door. Walking through the living room, he will mutter, "Oh. Kitty. You're right there."

Of course we were.

"Were you there the whole time?"

Indeed we were.

"Why did I not see you there before?"

It's obvious, isn't it? He did not see us because we were invisible.

"Well," he says, "good night." And now we no longer need our invisibility because he has turned off the light, and every cat knows that Laps have lousy eyesight. Especially in the dark.

So we remain visible.

We may levitate while sleeping, but the Laps rarely notice this unless they are children. The children sometimes notice as infants. They notice before they know that it is not usual for creatures to levitate. Then they stop noticing.

Laps of a certain age are capable of ignoring almost anything they set their minds to ignoring.

FELINITY

The path to inner peace?

Felinity.

Here's how: Simply allow yourself to be as you are. We are always as we are. Never more, never less. We may catch birds and sleep on the big puffy chair, but we do not open the cat food bag for ourselves or fill the water bowl. We do not make the mortgage payments or drive the car. We do not open doors, and we do not clean the litter box.

We eat. We sleep. We hunt. We demand affection and ear rubs. These are all things essential to felinity and that make us who we are. If we have anxiety, it is because we are being forced out of our felinity by some other source. If we are kept awake, for instance, or are not allowed to hunt properly (even if we only hunt a ball of yarn, it is essential to keeping our sanity, and thus our felinity).

We therefore request that you allow us to be as we are. And we will allow you the same. In fact, we insist. Be who you are. Peace—yours, ours, and theirs—shall follow.

FAMILIAR

Even after our own kittens have come and gone, we retain some of our own mother with us, as our kittens will retain some of us with them. We can project the image of our mother onto our Laps. Onto the dog. Onto a stuffed animal, if need be, or a living-room chair. Thus the human, the dog, the stuffed animal, or the living-room chair become part *mother*. We are tremendously good at this projection. It gives us comfort and helps protect us from the most prolific killer of all species: loneliness. We therefore do not fear loneliness because we never have it. It may appear to some that we are solitary creatures, but this is not entirely true because we are never truly alone.

In similar fashion, we soak up companionship when it is offered. It becomes a part of us, and we are able to use it whenever the room, the world, is quiet—whenever the world seems to be without the companionship we've recorded. When we need to be with our kittens, we are with them. When we need to be with Kittengirl, she is there. When we wish to see the blur as Fly makes his way through the house, we see it. When we need to hear the voice of Mom saying, "Awww, Kitty," we hear this voice without delay.

As we grow older, this retained companionship builds. In this way we may become a part of almost any family and remain a member of our first family. We may become members of every family. It is the great wisdom of cats to never be apart from those we have loved and those who have loved us. We are always with them, even when physically or temporally separate.

We sometimes wonder how other species overcome their inability to perform this feat of connectedness. We sometimes wonder how humans manage to live as long as they do. We suspect that it is precisely their inability to overcome loneliness on their own that makes the company of a cat so valuable to them.

And being both charitable and loving creatures, this is what we continue to offer. You who are a cat familiar.

With our blessings. Go into the world, and go in peace.

ABOUT THE AUTHOR

TERRY BAIN (aka Scratch) wrote *We Are the Cat* against the wishes of his cat companion, Swiper, who is still offended that he wrote his first book (*You Are a Dog*—a Pacific Northwest bestseller) about the dog. He is a freelance writer and book designer, and keeps a cat blog at *http://wearethecat.com*. He lives in Spokane, Washington, with his cat (who is standing at the door, ready to go out again, thank you), his wife, three children, and two dogs.